Philotheoi

1

St Macarius
P R E S S

First Revised Reprint—August 2023
© 2023 St Macarius Press

Monastery of Saint Macarius
the Great
P.O. Box 2780
Cairo—Egypt

E-mail: info@stmacariuspress.com
Website: www. stmacariuspress.com
Telegram Channel: t.me/stmacariuspress
Facebook Page: www.facebook.com/stmacariuspress

Printed in the United States of America

All rights reserved.

No part of this publication may be reproduced, stored in a retrieval system, or transmitted in any form or by any means—electronic, mechanical, graphic, photocopy, recording, taping, information storage, or any other—without written permission of the Publisher.

Anba Epiphanius and the Spirit of Saint Macarius

Edited by

Monk Markos el Makari

St Macarius Press

Monastery of Saint Macarius the Great (Egypt)

ISBN
978-1-7350713-8-1

Library of Congress Control Number
2023942779

Edition
Markos el Makari

Cover Photo
Photo taken at Bose Monastery (Italy)
on May 21, 2016

Cover
David Georgy

Format
5" x 8"

Pages
148

CONTENTS

Contents	5
Abbreviations	7
Introduction	11
Chapter 1—The Monastic Quest of the Young Tādrus	17
Chapter 2—Monk Epiphanius	27
Chapter 3—Bishop and Abbot Epiphanius	37
Chapter 4—"The Spirit of Saint Macarius": The Spiritual Fatherhood of Anba Epiphanius	49
Chapter 5—Teachings on Which He Insisted	85
Chapter 6—Anba Epiphanius' Universe	107
Conclusion—Twice a Martyr, Twice a Witness	143

ABBREVIATIONS

A Face   *Anbā Ibīfāniyūs: Waǧhun Taǧallā Fīhi al-Ḥubb* [Anba Epiphanius: a Face on Which Love has Manifested Itself] (Cairo: Madrasat al-Iskandariyya, 2018¹)

Alphabetical John Wortley (ed.), *Give Me a Word: The Alphabetical Sayings of the Desert Fathers* (Yonkers, NY: St Vladimir's Seminary Press, 2014).

ANF   Alexander Roberts, James Donaldson et al. (eds.), *Ante-Nicene Fathers, Vols. 1-10* (Buffalo: NY, Christian Literature Publishing Co., 1885-1896).

Audiography Audiography of Father Matthew the Poor: *al-'Ab Mattā al-Miskīn 'Ab al-Barriyya al-Muʿaṣir* [Father Matthew the Poor: A Contemporary Desert Father: Arabic edition of the Proceedings of the International Conference on Matthew the Poor held at

	the Bose Monastery, 21-22 May 2016] (Wādī al-Naṭrūn: Monastery of St Macarius, 2018): 332-387.
Bustān	Anba Epiphanius (ed.), *Bustān al-Ruhbān* [The Garden of the Monks] (Wādī al-Naṭrūn: Monastery of St Macarius, 2013).
Gordius	Basil of Caesarea, "A Homily on the Martyr Gordius," in Pauline Allen et al. (eds.), *'Let Us Die That We May Live': Greek Homilies on Christian Martyrs from Asia Minor, Palestine and Syria (c. AD 350–AD 450)* (London and New York: Routledge, 2003): 56-66.
Ibīfāniyūs	*Al-Anbā Ibīfāniyūs Alladī 'Aḥabba Al-Rahbana: Taʿālīmuhu Wa-ʿIẓātuhu Wa-Kitābātuhu Al-Rahbāniyya* [Anba Epiphanius Who Loved Monasticism: Teachings, Homilies, and Monastic Writings] (Wādī al-Naṭrūn: Monastery of St Macarius, 2019).
Macarius	Mattā al-Miskīn, "Al-Qiddīs Maqāriyūs Šahṣiyya Zāhira Bi-ʿAnāṣir 'Insāniyya Yanbaġī 'An

	Yuqtadā Bihā" [Saint Macarius: a Personality Rich in Human Gestures to Imitate], in *Saint Mark Review* (Dec. 1976): 23-28.
NPNF	Philip Schaff et al. (eds.), *Nicene and Post-Nicene Fathers*, series 2, Vols. 1-14 (Buffalo, NY: Christian Literature Publishing Co., 1886-1900).
Paradise	Ernest A. Wallis Budge (ed.), *The Paradise of the Holy Fathers* (Syriac Collection), II (London: Chatto & Windus, 1907).
PG	J.-P. Migne (ed.), *Patrologiae cursus completus. Series graeca* (Paris-Turnhout, 1857-1866).
So Great	Anba Epiphanius, *So Great a Salvation* (Wādī al-Naṭrūn: Saint Macarius Press, 2020^2).
Spiritbearer	Tim Vivian (ed.), *Saint Macarius the Spiritbearer* (New York, NY: St Vladimir's Seminary Press, 2004).
Systematic	John Wortley (ed.), *The Book of the Elders: Sayings of the Desert Fathers, the Systematic Collection* (Collegeville, MI: Liturgical Press, 2012).

Tafsiliyya	*Abuna Mattā al-Miskīn: al-Sīra al-Tafṣīliyya* [Father Matthew the Poor: Detailed Biography] (Wādī al-Naṭrūn: Monastery of Saint Macarius, 2008).
Wadid	Wadid el Makari, "Mattā al-Miskīn wa-l-Ḥayāh al-Rahbāniyya," in *al-'Ab Mattā al-Miskīn 'Ab al-Barriyya al-Muʿāṣir* (Wādī al-Naṭrūn: Monastery of Saint Macarius, 2018): 117-126

INTRODUCTION

Just as we are always amazed when we always observe the sun, so too do we always keep fresh the memory of that man. The just man will always be remembered (Ps. 111:6), both among those on earth, for as long as earth exists, and in heaven, and with the just Judge.[1]

These words, written by Saint Basil the Great in a panegyric that he dedicated to the Cappadocian martyr Gordius of Caesarea (†ca. 314), seem to us to be the best way to remember our father, bishop and abbot Anba Epiphanius.[2] For his numerous spiritual children, both within the monastery and all over the

---

[1] *Gordius*: 67.

[2] I feel deeply indebted to Father Wadid el Macari and Father Barnabas el Macari for their invaluable contribution. I sincerely thank Olivia Soliman from Australia and all those who wished to remain anonymous and who have lovingly and patiently offered suggestions, revised, and corrected the drafts. Without them this book would not have seen the light of day.

INTRODUCTION

world, he is a sun of extraordinary holiness and justice that draws its wonder from "Him who sanctifies" (Heb. 2:11) and the only "Sun of Justice" (Mal. 3:20), our Lord Jesus Christ. Meditating on Anba Epiphanius' life always leaves us amazed at how he walked—consciously and totally—behind the slain Lamb. His only weapons were love, mercy, patience, meekness, and humility, and his only goal was the heavenly Jerusalem.

We believe that it is necessary to continue to look at this holy man with great fear and trembling, to contemplate what Saint Pachomius, the father of the *koinonía*, called 'an admirable vision,' as he recounted:

> One of the brethren asked me once, 'Tell us about one of the visions you have, so we can profit from it.' I replied to him, 'A sinner like me is not given visions. But if you want to have an admirable vision that can be really useful to you, I will indicate it to you. It is this: if you see a humble-hearted and pure man, this is the greatest of all visions because, through him, you see God, who is invisible. Do not ask, therefore, for a more excellent vision than this'.[3]

This book is intended to ponder Anba Epiphanius' life. Starting with his personal monastic research that characterized him from an early age, we will narrate the story of Epiphanius the monk and the abbot.

---

[3] Apothegm n° 78 in *Bustān*, 50.

INTRODUCTION

Since the monastic life is first and foremost a lived 'life,' it is impossible to talk about monasticism in an abstract sense, as one risks missing the coordinates of 'life' and might find himself doing a philosophical exercise. The monks of the Egyptian desert have spoken of monasticism from their own personal experience and have seen with some suspicion any type of systematization of either the spiritual or the monastic life, even when it has been a question of refined attempts, such as those made by Evagrius Ponticus or by John Climacus.[4]

The fact that monasticism is a lived 'life' means that we are faced with "a relationship of intense and boundless love for Christ"[5] and, consequently, "a true and authentic death to the world, that is, to oneself,"[6] lived in everyday life.

As such, this 'life' concerns a personal experience embodied within a concrete monastic reality. In the words of Father Matthew the Poor, "the monastic community in which the monk lives is for him the

---

[4] Cf. Mattā al-Miskīn, *al-Rahbana al-Qibṭiyya Fī 'Aṣr al-Qiddīs Anbā Maqār* [The Coptic Monasticism at the Time of Saint Macarius] (Wādī al-Naṭrūn: St. Macarius Monastery, 2017): 130, 185-186, and Evelyn White, *The Monasteries of the Wadi n-Natrun*, part II (New York, NY: Metropolitan Museum of Art, 1932): 84.

[5] *Wadid*: 117.

[6] Mattā al-Miskīn, *Naṣā'iḥ Li-Ruhbān Ǧudud* (Wādī al-Naṭrūn: Monastery of St Macarius, 2012): 3.

INTRODUCTION

arena in which he submits to the death of the self."[7] For Anba Epiphanius, as well as for his spiritual guide, Father Matthew the Poor, monasticism is therefore situated at the confluence between the revelation of God's love, the experiential datum, and the constant dialogue with others' experiences, particularly those of the elders of today and of the early desert fathers. Anba Epiphanius' meditation on monasticism is the fruit of his sincere experience, embodying these three elements that we have outlined now. Although starting from his existential datum, which maintains relevance, the Egyptian abbot does not allow himself to go to an extremist existentialism. On the contrary, he constantly dialogued in a spirit of obedience with the living elders, experts in the art of monasticism, and rectified his experience in the light of the early monastic fathers. Although his monastic life as a simple monk and as an abbot might appear to be separate to one another, there are numerous common features which this book will try to highlight. The wonder of this bishop and abbot is that he managed, despite powerful opposing forces, to remain a monk, even as a superior.

We will begin by sketching, as best as an observer can, Anba Epiphanius' two main monastic phases, highlighting his spiritual connection with both Saint

---

[7] *Ibid.*

INTRODUCTION

Macarius and Father Matthew the Poor. We will then try to offer a synthesis of his major monastic themes, those *leitmotifs* on which he constantly insisted as an abbot, and which are also based in his long experience as a simple monk. The account of his monastic experience clarifies his insistence on certain teachings, and at the same time, explicitly outline what he always lived for. It is extraordinary to see how this man, as a monk as well as an abbot, was always profoundly consistent with himself.

Before we journey in better understanding the figure of Anba Epiphanius, it is worth pointing out that these pages are rich in questions and aspects of the Christian life that are understandable and applicable particularly to those who live a monastic life. However, its deeply evangelic content means that every Christian can benefit from it.

> Whoever desires to come after Me, let him deny himself, and take up his cross, and follow Me (Mark 8:34).

> If anyone comes to Me and does not hate his father and mother, wife and children, brothers and sisters, yes, and his own life also, he cannot be My disciple (Luke 14:26).

These verses, as well as others, are not taken from a 'manual for monks,' but from the Gospel. Therefore, they are addressed to every Christian who, in baptism, accepted to die to themselves with Christ in order to rise with Him to a new life.

INTRODUCTION

Finally, we would like to point out that, now and then, this book will occasionally include words in spoken Egyptian Arabic that are uncommon for the English-speaking reader and are terms specific to the world they portray, the Coptic Orthodox Church in Egypt. It is impossible to relate properly to Coptic Christianity without understanding this world.

And to the Lord of martyrs is due glory, honor, power and adoration, to the Father, to the Son and to the Holy Spirit, now and always, and forever and ever. Amen.

CHAPTER 1
THE MONASTIC QUEST
OF THE YOUNG TĀDRUS

We only know the basics of Anba Epiphanius' life before joining the monastery. He was born on June 27, 1954, in Ṭanṭā, a town in the Nile Delta halfway between the Rosetta branch (west) and the Damietta branch (east), to a religious family. Many of his relatives chose a consecrated life in the priesthood. The young Tādrus Zakī Tādrus Ǧirgis, the second of five children, was nurtured as a Christian in the church of Saint George the Great Martyr in the al-Ḥumra district of Ṭanṭā[1] since childhood, where he also met a servant who connected him to the Monastery of Saint Macarius.

The mildness and discretion of the young Tādrus were soon noticed by the bishop of the governorate of al-Ġarbiyya, Anba Yū'annis (1923–1987), a charismatic man of deep spirituality and vast culture whose work is still little known to the English-

---

[1] This is not the church that was bombed on Palm Sunday, April 9, 2017. The bombing happened at the church of Saint George located in the Abū al-Naǧā district of Ṭanṭā.

CHAPTER 1

speaking world.[2] Anba Epiphanius always kept an extraordinary memory of him, and, as a bishop, he repeatedly expressed his deep gratitude to him for encouraging him in his choice to become a monk. He considered him to be his mentor during the phase preceding his entry into the monastery, a role that was then fathered by Father Matthew the Poor. Anba Yū'annis also had great respect for the young Tādrus. When he discovered his intense passion for reading and studying, he encouraged him to join the Theological Seminary in Ṭanṭa. He also assigned him the task of organizing and managing both the library in Saint Paul's Cathedral in Ṭanṭa, as well as his own personal library. In this way, for the first time, the young Tādrus had access to a whole series of important texts in Arabic, including the apologetic publications of the early twentieth century, from whose denominational zealotry he soon distanced himself.

Even decades after the years Anba Epiphanius spent in the company of his father, teacher, and guide Anba Yu'annis, he often recounted a particular a scene that had a great impact on his spiritual life.

It happened one evening that he was among the group of deacons who prayed the midnight praises at Saint Paul's Cathedral in Ṭanṭa, which was under

---

[2] Saint Shenouda Press has published four volumes of his teachings.

construction at the time, and this coincided with the return of Anba Yu'annis from his weekly meeting in the city of Maḥalla al-Kubrā. When Anba Yu'annis heard the sound of praising, he entered the church, and he led the choir with his melodious voice. When the service ended, everyone started to leave the church and Anba Yu'annis walked ahead of those in attendance. Then, one of the church servants went to greet his disciple. The bishop turned towards the servant and said:

> Son, don't you know that you are still in the church that is called in the liturgy 'the house of the angels'? Even if it is empty and has no service or believers, it is full of angels, even if we do not see them with our physical eyes. It is appropriate for us to offer words of love and welcome to our loved ones outside the church. Let us maintain the spirit of prayer.'[3]

Anba Epiphanius often mentioned this scene to his spiritual children, because for him, it was the cornerstone of his liturgical ethics. According to him, there is no true liturgy without sincere respect for the church space, which is practically translated into maintaining complete silence, and keeping one's attention towards the celebrated mystery. He often used to say:

---

[3] From a conversation with one of Anba Epiphanius' close friends, currently a monk of the monastery.

CHAPTER 1

If you want to experience the Kingdom of Heaven in the Liturgy, preserve the sanctity and respect of the place.

His discipleship *ante litteram* towards Father Matthew the Poor and the Macarian spirituality began in the period between the end of high school and his first years at university. In the years 1971/2 Tādrus made the acquaintance of a young deacon from Alexandria, Magdī Anīs, who invited him to go on a pilgrimage to the monasteries of Wādī al-Naṭrūn. The young man, on the threshold of university, accepted the offer along with some other peers. At that time, venturing on a journey to reach Scetis[4] was rather difficult. The current Cairo-Alexandria highway was little more than a county road surrounded—and

---

[4] Saint Macarius was the initiator of the monastic life in Scetis where he arrived around 330 AD. John Cassian (*Conferences* 15:3,1) widely confirms it. Scetis is a desert depression (about 23 meters below sea level) about 60 kms long, located in the governorate of al-Buḥayra (Egypt), about 90 kms north-west of Cairo. The Arabic name, Wādī al-Naṭrūn, means the 'Natron *wadi*,' due to the presence in the surrounding area of different lakes containing nitrates, in particular a special salt, the 'natron' precisely, used above all for the mummification of bodies. The Coptic name, Ϣⲓϩⲏⲧ or Ϣⲓⲏⲧ, 'Scetis,' means 'scale of the heart.' In the Apothegms of the Desert Fathers, Scetis is sometimes called 'the great desert' (*panérēmos*) (cf. *Alphabetical Collection*, Macarius 3: "When Abba Macarius lived in the great desert (*en tē panérēmō*), he was all alone there, in total *anachoresis*"; translated from the Greek).

often submerged—by sand, devoid of any signs, or streetlights, meaning there was a high risk of accidents if one was not careful. Furthermore, in order to reach Saint Macarius' Monastery, the six-kilometer paved avenue that exists today, connecting the historic monastery to the current highway, was not yet paved. At the end of 1972, the first simple dirt road was created in the middle of the desert. Those who came from Ṭanṭā by public transport, as in the case of Tādrus, had to travel for at least six hours, if all went well, plus one hour to traverse the dirt road on foot. Only twice a day a bus would pass the monastery's gate from al-Ḥaṭāṭba town and thus one would risk missing it. However, Tādrus' eagerness to visit the monasteries, particularly the Monastery of Saint Macarius, had already been sparked through his biological father introducing him to the published works of Father Matthew the Poor, making this journey was one he was willing to traverse. He had been reading these texts since high school, in particular his volume on prayer, *Ḥayāt al-Ṣalāh al-'Urṯūḏuksiyya*,[5] originally published in 1952. Tādrus' family, who rarely saw him but for short moments after he joined the monastery, remember him for his inextinguishable thirst for knowledge as a voracious reader, especially the works of Father Matthew the Poor, and for having

---

[5] English translation: Matthew the Poor, *Orthodox Prayer Life* (Crestwood, NY: St Vladimir Press, 2003).

CHAPTER 1

enthusiastically completed reading the voluminous study dedicated by the latter to Saint Athanasius,[6] in just three days. On that first visit to the monasteries, Saint Macarius was left to last, after al-Baramūs, Saint Bišōī, and al-Suriyān. As soon as he entered, Tādrus found monks fatigued by the task of restoring the monastery, which had just begun, however they still showed bright and peaceful faces. His readings of the spiritual father of the monastery and his experience in person of the life in the monastery gave Tādrus the certainty that this place had something unique, and his heart became inextricably linked to it. From then on, pilgrimages and retreats to Saint Macarius' Monastery became a regular occurrence, initially with Magdī Anīs, and then alone or with a friend. His time at Saint Macarius Monastery made him fall in love with the *tasbiḥa*, the midnight prayer of praise in the Coptic tradition, which was not practiced in town at the time. Saint Macarius' *tasbiḥa* was distinctive with regard to the practices of the other monasteries for two main reasons. First, the adoption of a cadenced

---

[6] Cf. Mattā al-Miskīn, *Al-Qiddīs 'Aṯanāsiyūs Al-Rasūlī Al-Bābā Al-'Iśrūn (296-373): Sīratuhu, Difā'uhu 'An Al-Īmān Ḍidd Al-'Ariyūsiyyīn, Lāhūtuhu* [Saint Athanasius the Apostolic, the Twentieth Pope (296-373): Biography, Defense of the Faith Against the Arians, Theology] (Wādī al-Naṭrūn: Monastery of Saint Macarius, 1981). The volume, of about eight hundred pages, is considered all today as the best study in Arabic on the Father of the Alexandrian Church.

and meditative rhythm; and second, the freedom with which the parts to sing were chosen, avoiding rushing through the entirety of the prayer. Furthermore, at that time, the choir of the community—which did not exceed thirty monks—was very disciplined, and prayer was done by candlelight. All this was extremely suggestive.

In fact, it is worth noting that forty years later in 2013, when the monks chose Anba Epiphanius as their abbot, His Holiness Pope Tawadros II asked to meet him to get to know him better before entrusting him with the position. This meeting took place on February 26, 2013. When asked why he had chosen the Monastery of Saint Macarius to become a monk, Anba Epiphanius replied that the choice was dictated by two reasons: the midnight praises of the monastery, and the writings of Father Matthew the Poor.[7]

Back in the seventies, during their retreats in Saint Macarius, Tādrus and some of his friends did their best to memorize the *tasbiḥa*, even managing to recover an early rudimentary recording of the praises which they brought to Ṭanṭā. Through that cassette tape, the youngsters managed to revive the youth meeting in town, creating a fixed weekly appointment on Thursdays to gather and pray together. The number of young people, enthusiastic about what

---

[7] From a private conversation with Anba Epiphanius on September 19, 2015.

CHAPTER 1

was now called "Saint Macarius' *tasbiḥa*," grew so much that two choirs were created, one for men and one for women, who sang alternately.

The first face-to-face meeting with Father Matthew the Poor took place during Holy Week of 1974. One evening, while Fr Matthew was retiring to his cell and Tādrus was on a retreat at the monastery, Father Matthew asked who was currently housed in the *qaṣr*—the small guesthouse of the time. After being told that there was a group of college students, he decided to go up to the guest floor and talk to them about how the Holy Scripture had shaped his monastic life. Tādrus, now in his early twenties, did not know that he would attend one of the rare and most beautiful homilies Father Matthew ever delivered to the youth. That talk, which lasted a whole hour, was later given the title *Taʾṯīr al-'Inǧīl fī Ḥayātihi al-Rahbāniyya* (The Impact of Scripture on the Monastic Life of Father Matthew the Poor),[8] and became very well known. At the end of his homily, Father Matthew asked the students whether they knew two important hymns of Holy Week: *Ō Monogenēs* and *Pekthronos*. A few hands raised timidly. Father Matthew then said:

> How is this possible? Then it means that we must make you stay here and teach you all the long hymns. And I

---

[8] Recording MM-44 (cf. *Audiography*: 332-387).

am sure there will be monks among you. Do you think we labor in vain with you?[9]

He laughed and left. Of that group, six became monks in different years. Among them, Tādrus.

While the desire to become a monk in the monastery that he loved did not waver, Tādrus applied himself to finishing his studies without anyone knowing his true intentions. In 1978 he obtained a Bachelor of Medicine and Surgery from the University of Ṭantā, starting medical training at the Otolaryngology Division, first as a practitioner (1979), then as a physician assistant in a medical guard in the countryside of the governorate of al-Daqahliyya (1980-1981), and then as a resident doctor at Sūhāǧ University Hospital (1982-1983). Tādrus had to travel often as part of his medical training. He often found himself in challenging environments, in places where sin seemed open for many people. He mentioned that what protected him against temptation during that period were his father's prayers according to the flesh.

At the end of 1983, he enrolled in specialization courses at the University of Banhā, but he was overcome by the desire to leave. He never attended the lectures. In fact, a few months later, he sold everything he had, with the intention of settling in the Monastery of Saint Macarius.

---

[9] Conversation with one of those present, currently a monk of the monastery.

CHAPTER 1

Among these uplifting accounts of Tādrus' entry into the monastery is the story surrounding his decision to close his bank account. While he still did not know whether he would be accepted into the monastery or not, he entered the bank and asked the teller to close the account. The employee replied, "What a great pity! Why on earth do you want to close it?" He answered, "I am going to travel abroad!" The employee replied, "It must certainly be an invitation!"[10] And Tādrus said, "Yes, it is! It is exactly an invitation."[11]

---

[10] In Arabic the word *daʿwa* means both 'invitation' and 'vocation.' By *daʿwa* the bank teller meant an invitation made by a foreign citizen that allows an Egyptian citizen to easily obtain an entry visa. Anba Epiphanius, of course, meant *daʿwa* in the sense of God's vocation...

[11] The anecdote is reported by Father Arsanius el Makari in the introduction to *Ibīfāniyūs*: 7.

CHAPTER 2
MONK EPIPHANIUS

It is hard to investigate the deep motivations that drive a person to become a monk. Certainly, for Anba Epiphanius, the choice was confirmed in his adult years, especially after his attendance at the Monastery of Saint Macarius. To choose this monastery, especially at that time, meant the impossibility of following paths alternative or parallel to monasticism, such as ecclesiastical careerism or priestly services in parishes. If one wanted to become a monk-priest, which had become common practice in other monasteries, the Monastery of Saint Macarius was by no means the right place to join since the trait that most distinguished Saint Macarius from the other monasteries was the fact that the vocation of the community was exclusively monastic with limited monk-priests to serve the liturgical needs of the community. In fact, the three pillars of the monasticism of Saint Macarius'—as conceived by Father Matthew the Poor—were represented by a life of continuous prayer and serious and demanding work; fraternal love as the

CHAPTER 2

foundation of community life; and the refusal of the clericalization of the community.[1]

Tādrus' entry into the monastery took place on Saturday, February 18, 1984, after having attended the monastery as a guest for more than ten years. A few weeks after the beginning of his monastic journey, his family, who had been taken by surprise at his radical decision, came to see him. In his family, many of his cousins had indeed been called to priesthood, but none had opted for monasticism, which requires cutting off family ties. His father, worried about the fate of his son, asked him, "Can I leave you some money?" 'Aḫ[2] Tādrus replied, "For what?" And his father replied, "I am still your father!" The young man replied with the ardent zeal typical of novices, "I am dead, and you are dead! You are no longer my father!" It was a shock for his father and his family! Years later, a mature Anba Epiphanius, while admitting the severity of his words, recognized the beneficial effect that these had in the long run in the relationship between him and his family:

> My family members became monks themselves and helped me as a monk. They never intruded into my life

---

[1] Cf. *Tafsiliyya*: 244-255.
[2] In current practice, the term *'aḫ* 'brother' is placed before the name of the novice.

in the monastery, and after that episode, I never had to face spiritual struggles due to them.³

Anba Epiphanius joined the monastery in a historical time that many recognize as the 'golden age' of the community. There was intense activity in the monastery as its reconstruction was underway, and the monks spent many hours a day at work. Spiritual life was also in its splendor, for a variety of reasons.

First and foremost, the presence of Father Matthew the Poor in the community meant the monks were daily offered his long teachings on the Gospel and monastic life.⁴ Furthermore, when he was present in the monastery, every opportunity could be taken to create impromptu spiritual meetings in the courtyards and paths of the monastery. It was enough that a question from a monk required a slightly more complex answer that many monks thirsty to listen would flock around Father Matthew. The presence of Father Matthew did not mean that the community was a 'paradise' on earth, but it certainly was, as Anba Epiphanius would describe it, 'disciplined.'

Another element not to be underestimated was that the community at the time was smaller than it is now, with around ninety monks (currently the

---

³ *Ibīfāniyūs*: 7-8. Anba Epiphanius means spiritual struggles coming from yearning for the original family.

⁴ These catecheses have almost all been recorded and to a small extent also published. Cf. *Audiography*.

CHAPTER 2

monastery has one hundred and fifteen monks), and they were all gathered around the charismatic figure of Father Matthew the Poor. This helped the monastery live a real brotherhood, as one body and one spirit, called to the one hope of vocation (cf. Eph. 4:4). In those years, there lived many holy monks who, simply by their presence, helped the whole community remain focused on the ultimate purpose for which they had left the world.

Finally, at the time, it was very difficult to get to the monastery, and, generally, few people were allowed to visit. Father Matthew the Poor was very keen to preserve the peace of the monks, especially considering the fact that during the day, they were often busy with various, demanding jobs. He also feared that opening the monastery without control would irreparably compromise the monastic life. Therefore, the small community, the support of holy monks, the seriousness of the work and spiritual life of the individual monks, the reduced number of guests, and the mere presence of the spiritual father, Father Matthew, were all elements that encouraged the monks to maintain an atmosphere of a thorough spiritual focus.

The novitiate was brief when Anba Epiphanius joined the monastery. In fact, after only two months, on April 21, 1984, which coincided with Bright

MONK EPIPHANIUS

Saturday, he was ordained a monk[5] receiving the name Epiphanius. His task at the monastery for a long time was the breeding of hens. But soon, due to his many gifts, he was asked to hold several important positions in the monastery.

His affability and secular training positioned him to treat and serve the sick, not only within the walls of the monastery, but especially when it was necessary to travel outside the monastery. In 1997, he was asked to accompany his spiritual father, Father Matthew the Poor, as a physician during his trip to the United States, as Father Matthew had to undergo a delicate open-heart surgery. On that journey, which lasted about two months, the then *Abuna* Epiphanius got to know his spiritual father better, particularly through encountering his most humane and fragile self under the circumstances. It was an experience that profoundly marked his monastic journey, and which he jealously guarded when he returned to the monastery.

As well as Father Matthew, in 2002, Father Epiphanius accompanied Father Yūḥannā († 2021) to Germany for an angioplasty operation, and in 2008, he also accompanied Fathers Lūqā († 2009) and

---

[5] In the Coptic Orthodox Church, one speaks of *Risāma Rahbāniyya* 'monastic ordination.' *Risāma* is the ecclesiastical term also used for ordinations for all grades of the diaconate and the priesthood, including papal ordination.

CHAPTER 2

Panaghias († 2011) to Germany for cancer treatment. Within Egypt, he continued to treat the latter two monks with great devotion until the moment of their departure. The role of a physician allowed him to come into direct contact with the suffering Christ, seeing the words on the mystique of the Cross—that he had learned from his spiritual father—materialize daily. Serving the least, the weakest and most fragile members of the monastery taught him patience and humility, two virtues that he would later use most notably during his episcopate.

The monk Epiphanius was also endowed with refined intellectual qualities, which, since he joined the monastery, did not go unnoticed by Father Matthew the Poor. As a novice, he encouraged him to study the Fathers and the Tradition of the Church, and pointed out to him a whole series of fundamental readings, both in Arabic and English. A text of contemporary Orthodox theology that particularly nourished him was the book by Vladimir Lossky, *The Mystical Theology of the Eastern Church*, which seemed, in many ways, to be convergent with the Alexandrian mystical theology in general, and with Father Matthew's in particular. Years later, he recalled how he considered that text to be a fundamental introduction to understanding the richness of the theological heritage of the Christian East, and he encouraged others to read it.

MONK EPIPHANIUS

The young monk's love for Scripture and Tradition meant he immersed himself for hours in reading ancient patristic and monastic literature, and liturgical studies. His great love for reading, which accompanied him from a young age, led Father Matthew to appoint him as the librarian of the two libraries of the monastery; the Arabic library and the one for foreign languages.

Anba Epiphanius was an extremely punctual and faithful librarian. He was responsible for the digitalization of the paper catalog and the acquisition of important volumes. As a librarian, he had the opportunity to meet numerous personalities passing through the monastery. Everyone was able to test the affability, availability, and openness that were expressed in his welcoming and inimitable smile. Coptologist Father Philippe Luisier wrote:

> I met him when he was a librarian, then I saw him again when he became an abbot and bishop. He was always the same as himself, with this smile that is only his.[6]

Finally, it must be said that, as a bishop, he did not want to completely abandon his work as a librarian for the joy it gave him. It is due to him and his desire to spread knowledge that the beginning of the

---

[6] From an email correspondence with the monastery in August 2018.

CHAPTER 2

digitization process of the monastery's manuscripts was undertaken.

Because of his meticulousness, he was also asked by his spiritual father to take care of the finances of the monastery. From the early 1990s to the end of his life, he devoted himself totally to this rather thankless task. In 2015, he claimed that accepting that position, despite not having any accounting skills, taught him the profound value of obedience:

> By obeying, I perceived that the Lord was helping me. I tell you sincerely, without arrogance. I felt that the Lord was working with me. So much so that the bank's director we deal with came to the monastery and praised me in front of *abuna* [Matthew the Poor] saying, 'This monk is one of the best bursars I've ever dealt with!'[7]

In addition, Father Epiphanius worked for a period in the monastery's printing house, in the photocomposition department. Due to his accuracy and excellent knowledge of classical Arabic, he was soon requested to be a reviewer of the monastery's printing house. Working at the publishing house, he was also able to contribute as an author to the monastery's periodical, *Saint Mark*. It is in this writing workshop that the seeds were planted for some of his works

---

[7] This was said on the occasion of a monastic conference with the novices of the Monastery of Bose (Italy), September 10, 2015.

published after his ordination as an abbot. These texts mainly consist of his biblical meditations, as well as his studies of the writings of the well-known Arab-Christian author Būlus al-Būšī.

In 2002, when the monks in charge of celebrating the liturgy began to age, Father Matthew the Poor, in order to relieve the load of the elders, chose some monks to be ordained priests. Among these was Father Epiphanius, though he asked tearfully to be exempted because of his unworthiness, yet obedience compelled him to accept this ordination. Due to his simplicity and spirituality, the choice to concelebrate with our *rubbēta*[8] at the time, Father Kyrillos (✝ 2012), fell on him and on Father Panaghias, on the occasion of the great feasts and most of the Sundays of the year. At the end of each celebration, Father Panaghias, to shake off any feelings of vainglory, used to run to the barn to milk the cows. Similarly, Father Epiphanius went around the monastery, offering his services to the humblest of recipients, and to anyone who needed them.

---

[8] *Rubbēta* is an Egyptian word of Syriac origin (*rab baytā*, lit. 'house master'). In Coptic monasticism, this figure indicates the monk in charge of organizing and coordinating the monastery's daily affairs. The *Rubbēta* is the second office of the monastery after the abbot, who is also a bishop in the monasteries today. To make a comparison with Western monasticism, the *Rubbēta* is similar to a prior with functions of treasurer, where the monastery is presided over by an abbot.

CHAPTER 3
BISHOP AND ABBOT EPIPHANIUS

On February 3, 2013, the newly elected Coptic Patriarch, His Holiness Pope Tawadros II, asked the monks of the monastery to vote on the abbot to be chosen within the monastery's community. The vote, in which more than one hundred monks participated, took place in the presence of the personal secretary of Pope Tawadros at the time, Father Angelos Isḥaq. On the first of March 2013, an official statement from the Papal Headquarters arrived at the monastery, announcing the end of vote counting and that the monk-priest Epiphanius had obtained the majority of votes. The choice of the monastery was blessed, through a recommendation, by Metropolitan Miḫa'īl (1921–2014), who was at the time the Metropolitan of Asyūṭ and had been the abbot of the monastery for about sixty-five years. He had asked Pope Tawadros shortly before to ordain a new bishop for the monastery in his place. In the previously mentioned private meeting between Father Epiphanius and His Holiness Pope Tawadros II, which was held on February 26, 2013, His Holiness recommended that he "restore

CHAPTER 3

the ancient luminous face of the Monastery of Saint Macarius and reunite the community." His Holiness publicly repeated the same recommendation at the time of Anba Epiphanius' ordination as a bishop and abbot on March 10, 2013. Since he was the first bishop ordained by His Holiness Pope Tawadros II, the Patriarch repeatedly referred to him as "the first fruit of my ordinations." On March 18, 2013, the new superior of the monastery, Anba Epiphanius, was enthroned in the presence of more than forty bishops and metropolitans. Shortly after the election, Bishop Epiphanius addressed a message to the community of Saint Macarius, which reads as follows:

Dear Fathers and Brothers,

Peace and love of our Lord Jesus Christ.

I thank the Lord Jesus Christ for the grace He endowed me with, without having any merit, to be a servant of this monastery.

I thank His Holiness the Pope for his interest in our monastery, and I also thank His Eminence Metropolitan Mīḫāʾīl for his recommendation and prayers for us.

I thank all of you for the feelings of love that you have shown me, and I especially thank our holy Father Isidore, who led the monastery throughout the past period with all love and in which he sacrificed his own comfort for that of the fathers.

BISHOP AND ABBOT EPIPHANIUS

And I thank our holy Father Petronius for his agreement to take over the administration of the monastery in the coming period.

You know the recommendations that His Holiness the Pope gave us for the return of the monastery to its luminous face which is the responsibility of all monks before His Holiness, the whole Church, and also all the monastic saints who look to us and support us with their prayers so that we follow in the footsteps of their monastic teachings.

I hope that you will always remember me in your prayers, so that the Lord will grant me the blessing to serve this monastery and so that we may gladden the hearts of our fathers, the saints of this place, with our faithfulness to the monastic commandments that they handed down to us.

Your brother,

Epiphanius

Our father Epiphanius maintained this humble style of addressing the monks of his monastery, calling himself "your brother" throughout his abbacy until the day of his departure. He considered that the leadership of the monastery was a service and a sacrifice that he offered to his brethren more than anything else. He imitated in this his divine Teacher, who said about Himself, "…the Son of Man did not come to be served, but to serve, and to give his life as a ransom for many" (Matt 20:28).

CHAPTER 3

For the sake of this service, he was content to sacrifice his personal comfort. Over the five years in which he led the monastery, he did not turn off his phone day or night, no matter how tired he was. He used to say to the monks of his monastery on many occasions, "My phone is on day and night for every monk who needs me." The cost of this sacrifice cannot be estimated, until one considers that when he was a monk, he used to go to bed at 8:30 in the evening, turn off his phone, and prevent anyone from knocking on his door. However, when he became a bishop, he felt that he was indebted to all the monks of his monastery, not only by opening his phone, but by opening his heart, offering to patiently listen to everyone at all times, and welcoming and comforting every tired monk.

Once, our beloved abbot came late to the daily meal at the refectory. He arrived after the end of the ninth hour prayer and barely gave the blessing and read from the *Bustān al-Ruhbān* (The Monks' Garden).[1] He was asked, "Why were you late today, *sayyidna*?" He replied, "I stayed with a monk for three hours at his work. He kept complaining and criticizing everything, and I tried to comfort him and win him over with love. I could not leave him before I

---

[1] The Copto-Arabic collection of apothegms of the Desert Fathers.

was assured that my love had reached his heart and that his soul had been calmed."

After his ordination as a bishop, the monks began to notice how Anba Epiphanius—to use the previously quoted words of Father Luisier—"had always remained the same." He never accepted *metanoias*[2] be done to him and to those who insisted he used to say, "If you prostrate yourself in front of me, I will do the same with you!" or, jokingly, "If you bow down, I will not greet you anymore!" He never wore the so-called *'imma* in the monastery, the typical headcover of Coptic bishops, nor did he bear the pastoral staff. He wore the *'imma* for certain official or formal occasions but, as soon as the occasion was officially over, he did not let a single moment pass before he took it off and laid it down. For him, the *'imma* was like a wall imposed between him and others, while he would always try to put himself on the same level as others in order to be closer to them. Furthermore, he did not appreciate the honorary title of 'Excellency' or *sayyidnā*. He was very happy if someone simply called him *abūnā*, 'father.' He said that these high-sounding titles of 'Excellency,' *sayyidnā* etc. were extraneous to tradition and had stealthily entered the Coptic Church during the Ottoman domination.

---

[2] Prostrations to ask for the blessing.

CHAPTER 3

The community liturgy in the monastery was another space in which Anba Epiphanius tried to be the servant of all. He never sat on the episcopal seat (which, in the monastery, was only a simple armchair) but sat on the ground like the other monks. He refused to wear the bishop's liturgical clothes, rather he was content with a simple white tunic like the other celebrants. To those who asked him why he undertook such extreme sobriety, he replied, "These ornate vests are for eparchial bishops. In the monastery, we must keep our monastic simplicity."

He asked that the hymns in honor of the bishop not be sung for him during the liturgy in the monastery. The problem arose when he had to travel. On several occasions, Anba Epiphanius was seen going to great lengths to prevent the typical episcopal hymns from being sung for him, especially the processional hymn of *Ekesmaroout* (Blessed are you), which mentions the bishop's name as a concluding benediction. When he was outside of the monastery, he usually used to arrive much earlier than the time of the liturgy and was already found praying so that he could not be processed in. A Coptic liturgy was celebrated during the conference on Matthew the Poor in 2016 at the Monastery of Bose in Italy. At that time, Anba Epiphanius arrived very early at the church and started walking briskly close to the wall so as not to be seen by anyone. Yet, a deacon was already in the church, and so, as soon as he saw Anba Epiphanius, he started singing *Ekesmaroout* out loud. Anba Epiphanius did not appreciate at all and immediately told him to stop. In Melbourne, in 2018, entering a church, he refused to be processed in and instead walked through the deacons and ahead of them and opened the sanctuary's veil so they would not mention his name.

If a person did not know him, it was impossible to recognize him in the monastery as the abbot, both when he was around the monastery or when he presided over the Agpia prayers or the Divine Liturgy. Once, a married *qummuṣ*[3] came to visit the monastery and attended the Divine Liturgy over which Anba Epiphanius was presiding. At the moment of communion, according to liturgical practice, Anba Epiphanius, as a bishop, gave communion to all those present, including priests and *qamāmiṣa*[4] directly in their mouths as is customary in liturgy. When the turn of the said *qummuṣ* came, Anba Epiphanius was about to give him communion under the dome of the Sanctuary of Pope Benjamin in the Church of Saint

---

[3] The word *qummuṣ* derives from the Greek *hēgúmenos*. However, nowadays it does not indicate anymore the superior of a monastery. It is simply an honorific title granted to priests after many years of service. Married priests can also carry the title of *qummuṣ*.

[4] Plural of *qummuṣ*.

CHAPTER 3

Macarius. The *qummuṣ*, who did not know him, felt offended and immediately said to him, "I am a *qummuṣ*!" By this, he meant that a normal priest could not give him communion, but he had to give himself communion as a higher priestly rank. Anba Epiphanius kept silent while the *qummuṣ* communed and walked away. He then told a monk of the monastery what had happened, saying, "That monk-priest of yours wanted to give me communion today! Don't you know the rules in this monastery?" The monk replied, "Which monk-priest are you talking about? Today, the abbot, Anba Epiphanius, was presiding!" The *qummuṣ* became all colors and, having found Anba Epiphanius, apologized to him. Anba Epiphanius embraced him, smiling, without saying a word.

For the liturgies in which he had to anoint the assembly (such as, the Friday of the end of Lent and Bright Saturday), he did not wait for the faithful to go to him, but it was he who, taking the ampoule of oil, passed among the ranks and anointed each one in his place. Very often, when he presided over the vespers, we saw him standing deliberately in the middle of the rear choir and not in the front choir of the Church of Saint Apa Ischyron, where the monk-priest who leads the prayer normally stands. Anba Epiphanius lived in the community as a *neóteros* (the youngest) and a *diákonōn* (the one who serves) while being the *hēgúmenos* (the one who rules) and the

BISHOP AND ABBOT EPIPHANIUS

meizōn (the greatest; cf. Luke 22:26). He daily, concretely, embodied for the monks the One who said to his disciples, "…I am among you as the One who serves" (Luke 22:27). This provided him with a great deal of flexibility with his brethren. His sense of discernment, which he cultivated by always putting himself in the place of others, allowed him to never be rigid. Before making a decision, he listened intently and always tried to adapt to the person in front of him. He firmly believed that the superior of a monastery must be the same as the brethren in everything. Several times, he repeated to the monks the following saying of Pachomius:

> It is said of Saint Pachomius that he once did a job with his brethren and that such work required each of them to bring a large quantity of bread. One of the young men said to him, 'Never let it be that you bring anything, father. Behold, I bring what is enough for me and for you together.' The saint replied, 'God forbid! If it has been written of the Lord that he wanted to resemble his brethren in everything (cf. Heb. 2:17), how could I, the ignoble, distinguish myself from my brethren so as not to carry my load with them?'[5]

The refectory was a very important monastery space for Anba Epiphanius, which we will discuss later.[6] For now, two stories are of great significance.

---

[5] Apothegm n° 75, in *Bustān*: 48.
[6] See below: 499.

CHAPTER 3

Firstly, Anba Epiphanius was the author of an astounding gesture right in the refectory. This hall comprises a long table in the shape of a horseshoe where the monks normally sit on very low stools, according to their seniority. At the meeting point of the two branches of the table sits the lectern, where the sayings of the Desert Fathers are read daily. To the right of the lectern sit the older monks, while to the left sit the younger monks, with a seat right before the lectern for the abbot. After his election as an abbot, Anba Epiphanius' seat in the middle of the refectory's table had been prepared for him. With extreme simplicity, and a gesture that floored everyone, he took one of the small stools of the monks and his wooden nameplate, and sat down next to the last novice.

Secondly, he himself took great care in reading the apothegms of the Desert Fathers in the refectory every day to transmit to his monks the value of deep communion with previous generations. When he read to us, we felt that the boundaries of our community widened to contain hundreds of thousands of holy monks who lived before us and who, always alive, look at us from above, encouraging us, and living in communion with us, as "He is not the God of the dead, but of the living" (Luke 20:38). It was really moving to see how, after the five hours of the Sunday liturgy (most of which he spent standing...) having

BISHOP AND ABBOT EPIPHANIUS

blessed all the monks one by one, he quickly removed his liturgical vestments, in order not to keep the monks waiting, and, at a brisk pace, headed to the refectory in order to recite, out of breath, the blessing, before reading the apothegms.

Finally, he believed that his role as a bishop was first and foremost to preside over the one communal Divine Liturgy, the Sunday Liturgy,[7] which gathers all the monks around the one Bread, and distribute the Body and Blood of the Lord to them. For Anba Epiphanius, this was how he could best contribute to achieving the ultimate goal, not only of the coenobitic monasticism, but even that of the whole creation, to "…gather together in one all things in Christ" (Eph. 1:10). Therefore, he never missed Sunday liturgy, unless he was obliged for a trip or an illness, and

---

[7] Since the time of Father Matthew the Poor there has been a lot of insistence in the Monastery of Saint Macarius on the importance of the one community Divine Liturgy which brings together all the monks. In the annual (ordinary) liturgical time, it is celebrated only on Sunday and on the occasion of the saints' feasts. The prayers begin with midnight praise, at 2 am, and end with the actual Divine Liturgy. Exceptionally, during fasting periods, other Divine Liturgies are added: during minor fasts (the fast of the Nativity, the Apostles and the Virgin Mary) the community liturgy is also celebrated on Wednesdays and Fridays. Lent is a separate case. The Monastery of Saint Macarius in Lent celebrates the Eucharistic liturgy every day (except Saturdays), at times later than usual to allow monks and faithful to fast.

CHAPTER 3

he encouraged his monks to do the same. In this, he was a worthy successor of the bishops of the early centuries, such as Ignatius, Cyprian, Irenaeus and Peter of Alexandria. And like them, he ended his life with martyrdom.

CHAPTER 4
"THE SPIRIT OF SAINT MACARIUS": THE SPIRITUAL FATHERHOOD OF ANBA EPIPHANIUS

To understand Bishop Epiphanius' spiritual personality, we would like to evoke an image that can help us make our way into his heart.

The Monastery of Saint Macarius houses many relics: those of the three Macarii,[1] placed in three wooden cylinders, are of great importance, in particular the relics of Saint Macarius the Great, the founder of monasticism in Scetis. Other important relics include those of Saint John the Baptist, Forerunner of the Lord, of Saint Elisha the prophet, disciple of Elijah, and of Saint John Kolobós.[2] Anba Epiphanius seems to have obtained from God some of the spirit

---

[1] They are Macarius the Great (300—390), Macarius of Alexandria (300 ca.-395) and Macarius bishop of Tkaw († 451), whose relics lie in the main monastery's church of Saint Macarius the Great.

[2] John Kolobós (ca. 339-409), or 'the dwarf,' so called for his short stature, was one of the Desert Fathers, disciple of Abba Amoe. His relics rest in the church of Saint Apa Iskhyron.

CHAPTER 4

of these four saints. To an Australian priest who asked him in July 2018 what had changed in him after the abbacy, Anba Epiphanius explicitly said:

> The Lord gave me the spirit of Saint Macarius: I see people sin, and it is as if I did not see them.

This expression reflects a famous saying from Saint Macarius:

> They used to say of Abba Macarius the Great that he became "a god on earth", as it is written (cf. Ps. 81:6), for just as God overshadows the earth, so was Abba Macarius overshadowing shortcomings, as though not seeing what he saw and not hearing what he heard.[3]

So, the abbot of Saint Macarius' Monastery was aware that he had received the spirit of the great desert saint. Judging by his words and his life, this certainty supported him in his daily work as an abbot is evident.

In this, he resembles Saint Elisha, the beloved disciple of Elijah, who asked his teacher, before he was raptured into heaven on the chariot of fire, to have a double portion of his spirit (cf. 2 Kings 2:9). Anba Epiphanius, this modern Elisha, obtained the spirit of his father, Saint Macarius.

Furthermore, the life of Anba Epiphanius, in particular the last years in which he became a public figure, showed us how much he possessed, at least in

---

[3] Cf. *Alphabetical Collection*, Macarius 32 (*Alphabetical*: 188).

part, the spirit of John the Baptist. Anba Epiphanius did not have the strictness of the Baptist (although he certainly possessed his ascetic spirit), nor did he imagine Christ holding the winnowing fan in his hand to clean out the threshing floor from the wicked and burning the chaff with unquenchable fire (cf. Matt. 3:12). However, Anba Epiphanius, like John, never tried to take the place of Christ—"He confessed, and did not deny, and he confessed, 'I am not the Christ'" (John 1:20). In doing this, he always indicated the source of all good, Christ, in whom we have so great a salvation—"And looking at Jesus as He walked, he said, 'Behold the Lamb of God, who takes away the sin of the world!'" (John 1:36,29). Anba Epiphanius was the mild voice of one who cries 'from' the desert, hoping, until the very end, in the transformation of the wicked (cf. John 1:23). He was the living example of the words, "He must increase, but I must decrease" (John 3:30).

Saint John Kolobós is another of the saints of the monastery who deeply inspired Anba Epiphanius. This Desert Father became known for his numerous virtues, in particular for his great humility, obedience, patience, forbearance, and openness towards others.[4]

---

[4] For the Coptic and Syriac life of John Kolobós, see Maged S. A. Mikhail and Tim Vivian (eds.), *The Holy Workshop of Virtue: The Life of John the Little by Zacharias of Sakha* (Trappist, KY: Cistercian Publications, 2010).

CHAPTER 4

Anba Epiphanius certainly possessed all these virtues and his relationship with some of them—in particular humility, of which Saint John was a model—will be detailed below when talking about the figure of Saint Macarius. Here, it is important to highlight Anba Epiphanius' close link to Saint John Kolobós as both shared being despised by their own brethren. Like a new Joseph (Jacob's son of the Old Testament), Saint John had to endure the insult, neglect, envy, derision, and misunderstanding of many of his brethren. This link with Saint John's life clearly emerges from Anba Epiphanius' catecheses on Saint John.[5] It was an aspect that touched him so deeply that we can say, in retrospect, that the attention paid to it by Anba Epiphanius became a sort of prophecy about his own life. It is impressive to hear in one of his speeches, "Saint John was touched by the story of Joseph because he saw it reflected in his life and, for this reason, he spoke about it to his spiritual children in the desert."[6] The same was true for him since for Anba Epiphanius, Saint John was among the Desert Fathers who experienced, more than others, *kénōsis*, the self-emptying of which the Logos made flesh is the supreme model (cf. Phil. 2:7). By totally assimilating himself to Christ, who emptied Himself and died on

---

[5] In particular, the speech delivered to the monks on the occasion of the feast of Saint John Kolobós, October 30, 2016.

[6] *Ibid.*

the Cross, Saint John emptied himself and died on an invisible cross. A saying that was particularly close to Anba Epiphanius' heart reads:

> Once [John Kolobós] asked the brethren, 'Who sold Joseph?' They answered him, 'His brethren.' He said: 'It was not his brothers who sold him, but his humility. He could in fact tell the one who had bought him that he was their brother but kept silent and was sold for his humility. And with that same humility, he became administrator of the king of Egypt.'[7]

It was not the brothers who sold Joseph, but his humility and obedience to events that Saint John accepted as divine will. So it was for Anba Epiphanius who suffered at the hands of his brothers but, in reality, the real cause behind this suffering was his humility and obedience, which totally assimilated him to Joseph, John, and Christ. Anba Epiphanius could have had many ways out, but he decided to obey God's will to the point of giving up his life.

Yet, the reward for Saint John's emptying and death was a better resurrection (cf. Heb. 11:35). Of John, in fact, it is said, "Who is John who has the whole Scetis hanging on his little finger on account of his humility?"[8] The same goes for Anba Epiphanius, whose exceptional humility caused him

---

[7] Apothegm n° 240 in *Bustān*: 126.
[8] *Alphabetical Collection*, John Kolobós, 36 (*Alphabetical*: 139).

CHAPTER 4

suffering from some, but won him the love and appreciation of so many disciples from all around the world.

Therefore, Anba Epiphanius consciously placed himself on the path traced by these four saints. He took some traits from each of them, but judging by what he verbally expressed, we can say that he felt most invested in the spirit of Saint Macarius, a monk and a father of monks who was always deeply transparent with himself, made simplicity his daily compass, and refused to judge others. He always considered himself 'on the way' and not yet perfected, showing how mercy was an expression of *théōsis*, or deification,[9] while living as an eschatological being in anticipation of the *parousía* of Christ and the life of the world to come.

Bishop Epiphanius' abbacy, therefore, constantly looked at the spiritual work of Saint Macarius. It is not a coincidence that during his abbacy, the monastery published a translation of the second collection of Saint Macarius' homilies, translated into Arabic for the first time in the modern era directly from the original Greek text. He asked that the publication be part of a series called, "The Complete Works of Saint

---

[9] Cf. the section *Ecclesiological and Theological Vision* in this book, pp. 118-28.

"THE SPIRIT OF SAINT MACARIUS"

Macarius the Great," hoping that the monastery would continue this important task.

The monastic work of Father Matthew the Poor had previously looked at the same spiritual heritage. Father Matthew not only carried out an architectural re-foundation of the monastery, but he also inspired an intense spiritual rebirth, repositioning the monastery on the ancient Macarian trail through a return to the sources and spirit that animated the ancient monasticism of Scetis.

For many years, Anba Epiphanius had seen the spirit of Saint Macarius concretely realized through both the writings and the daily life of Father Matthew the Poor. It is interesting that Father Matthew the Poor said something very similar to what was expressed by Anba Epiphanius about the gifts that God had bestowed on him as superior of the monastery:

> With my peaceful and loving heart and my mild soul that knows no grudge, I patiently bear [with those who oppose me]. The hilt of the sword is in their hands. I, on the other hand, am unable to be cruel to anyone. I embrace my worst enemy like my brother, no matter what he does to me. This is a gift that God gave me.[10]

This spiritual sonship of Anba Epiphanius towards both the father of Scetis' monasticism and the one

---

[10] Conversation with some monks (July 1979), reported in *Tafsiliyya*: 316.

CHAPTER 4

who revived it is especially evident if one looks back at his spiritual fatherhood in the years of his abbacy. While many similarities bind these three monks of Scetis, the following pages trace some of their most significant commonalities.

1. Humility

Why did the abbot Anba Epiphanius want to live in the way that he did? Because he thought of himself as a simple monk and lived as a simple monk. This is an essential point in understanding his character, spirituality, and spiritual fatherhood.

His cell, to which he returned every evening (even when he was obliged by ecclesial and institutional commitments late into the night), is the most eloquent witness, since it was a small, austere, and essential space. When he took it over, having previously been the cell of Father Matthew the Poor, he was told that it was necessary to do some essential renovations because everything was stuck in the seventies! He categorically refused, insisting that "the cell must remain as it is."

In that cell, he always found his self-emptying, his abandonment of the world, and the profound aim of his monastic vocation. He also made concrete gestures to practice this, such as sleeping on the ground on a humble 'futon.' 'Monk' was the only 'title'—if one can call it that—which he accepted with joy,

"THE SPIRIT OF SAINT MACARIUS"

often with great emotion. Being a monk gave him enormous inner freedom; a freedom that clearly manifested itself to others. It is to maintain this impetus towards Christ and his neighbor that he often had this response to praise:

> Do not praise a monk in his face, otherwise, you hand him over to the devil.[11]

Paradoxically, we heard this phrase more when he was a bishop than when he was a simple monk, confirming how he truly saw himself. In speaking of his humility, three episodes during his abbacy particularly illustrate this.

As mentioned earlier, Anba Epiphanius insisted on continuing to work as a librarian because he deeply loved this work. Only three copies of the keys existed for the library: two were in the possession of the two other monks who helped him, and the other set was owned by him. One day, the two librarians were surprised by entering the library and finding it perfectly clean and swept. Looking to each other in amazement, they asked one another who had opened for cleaning. Both replied that they had not opened the library to anyone. They said, "It cannot be Anba Epiphanius, can it?" They remained in doubt for some days, until they discovered that it was Anba Epiphanius—the only one with the third set of keys—

---

[11] Cf. *Systematic Collection*, 21:54 (*Systematic*: 381)

CHAPTER 4

who had done the sweeping and tidying up of the library on his own.

One time, he was invited to deliver one of the inaugural lectures at a colloquium, and he took his place on the stage with other important personalities. However, the next day, he was seen sitting among the audience, towards the back. When invited to resume his place on the platform, he gave the answer, "Yesterday I was a speaker; today I came to learn."

Once, a family came to visit the monastery. Before the guests arrived, Anba Epiphanius remained in the kitchen with the monk in charge the whole time, arranging the food for them. When the guests were about to arrive, Anba Epiphanius asked the monk in charge of the kitchen to come with him to welcome them. Upon entering, the guests saw two simple monks, one in his thirties and one with a white beard. Anba Epiphanius was, in fact, dressed in a simple 'no-frills' *galabiyya*[12] and very regular plastic sandals that all the other monks normally wear. He had no pectoral cross to indicate that he was a bishop. The abbot warmly greeted the guests and offered them lunch and tea after which he offered them a spiritual word. At the end of the visit, when they were about to leave, they asked to greet the abbot. Anba Epiphanius' reply

---

[12] A traditional Egyptian garment. The Coptic clergy wear a black one.

"THE SPIRIT OF SAINT MACARIUS"

was, "What is the need to greet him? It's a waste of time!" The guests insisted, saying, "We have come this far, and we were expecting to meet him! We want to get his blessing!" Anba Epiphanius tried other ways to dissuade them. When they began to become adamant, he was forced to reveal his identity, to their enormous surprise.

A saying of Saint Macarius helps us understand how Anba Epiphanius followed in the footsteps of the father of Scetis' monasticism:

> They used to say of Abba Macarius that, if a brother approached him timidly as a great and holy elder, he would not say anything to him. But if one of the brothers spoke to him as though he were putting him down, 'Abba, when you were a camel-driver and you used to steal natron to sell it, did the guards not beat you?'—if somebody spoke to him like that, he would happily converse with him if he asked him anything.[13]

Father Matthew comments on this saying of Saint Macarius with these words:

> Saint Macarius refused to put on the halo because of his works, his asceticism, or his function as superior. Instead, he insisted on behaving with the same qualities and the same spirituality with which he had started his monastic life, first of all with himself and then with his spiritual children. Plainly said, Saint Macarius liked, deep down, to continue to consider himself a layman—

---

[13] *Alphabetical Collection*, Macarius 31 (*Alphabetical*: 188).

CHAPTER 4

a camel driver who steals the natron—and could not stand that his spiritual children deceive him or praise him as better than any layman. It is as if he wanted to tell us, 'All that is negative or weak in my life is mine, of Macarius, while all that is noble and exalted is from Christ who lives in me. How can I take what belongs to Christ and attribute it to me, or how can I take for myself the honor that belongs to Christ?' This principle with which Macarius lived among his children helps us better understand his personality—he was authentic without falsehood, and he did not like flattery. He lived his own reality in its most fragile condition, without denying the past or being proud of the successes of the present; he did not impose respect on his children for his function as superior. Indeed, he did not accept that his talents be made available to his relationship with his spiritual children and his disciples, but, in silence and extreme delicacy, he imposed on everyone that the dialogue and the relationship with them be based on his weakness and not on his strength... Macarius imposed this on his converser to avoid any ceremoniousness towards him, in order to erase from his soul any feeling of fear or awe so that he could live, appear, and speak in that simple and authentic way that he loved so much, like a simple camel driver traveling to his heavenly homeland.[14]

Father Seraphim of the Monastery of al-Baramūs comments on this by saying:

---

[14] *Macarius*: 23–24.

"THE SPIRIT OF SAINT MACARIUS"

Consciously or unconsciously, he never aspired to be a head other than the only Head, Christ. He was happy to be the companion of the others, united with them in the same hope as a member of the one Body. Only as a member, brother, or companion. Just as Saint John writes at the beginning of the Apocalypse, 'I, John, both your brother and companion in the tribulation and kingdom and patience of Jesus Christ' (Rev. 1:9). This is why I believe that he did not have to make an effort to be humble or simple with those around him. Being like this really represented a source of happiness for him. For this reason, he suffered and was annoyed if someone tried to raise him to a position that made him lose the pleasure of spontaneous communion with his brethren in the one Body.[15]

Father Matthew the Poor did not like when others gave him more importance than was strictly necessary either. He once said to the monks:

> God gives me, to enrich others, six or seven times as much information as He gives me personally. In my cell, He says to me, 'Open your mouth,' and then feeds me with the dropper! And I say, 'Lord, give me something more! Here we work like mills!' And he replies, 'No'... God has hidden me from the world but has taken my name and uses it for His work. In any case, I can see myself clearly, and I know myself perfectly and how much I am worth. When someone praises me, I do not

---

[15] *A Face*: 56.

CHAPTER 4

change my opinion of myself. In fact, I feel extremely embarrassed.[16]

It is known that, although many asked to meet him for the fame that spread in Egypt and around the world, Father Matthew usually did not consent, saying that he was not an important person. In a homily, he uttered:

> Beloved ones, there is a secret I want to reveal to you. I prayed to the Lord, asking him to allow me to enter and leave the church without anyone recognizing me. Many times, it happened that people did not recognize me. Many ask me, 'We want to see *abūnā Mattā*!' Once, someone approached me asking, 'Can I meet *abūnā Matta*?', and I replied, 'Absolutely not. He would not agree because he is arrogant! It is impossible to get him out of the cell!' So, the Lord hid me from people's eyes. We do not have to care if we are known in church or not. We must think only of our heavenly citizenship without wishing for anything on earth.[17]

This brings to mind the famous saying of Saint Macarius:

> Abba Macarius was once coming from the marsh to his own cell carrying reeds when the devil met him on the way, carrying a scythe; he wanted to strike him but could not. He said to him, 'There is a great force about

---

[16] Speech to the monks, September 3, 1982 (reported in *Tafsiliyya*: 309)

[17] From homily MM-49 (cf. *Audiography*).

"THE SPIRIT OF SAINT MACARIUS"

you Macarius, for I cannot get at you. See, whatever you do, I do it too. You fast, I do not eat at all; you keep watch, I do not ever sleep. There is only one thing in which you have the better of me.' 'What is that?' Abba Macarius said to him, and he said: 'Your humility; because of that I cannot get at you.'[18]

Like Saint Macarius, Anba Epiphanius and Father Matthew the Poor were clothed in this divine humility that allowed them to resist the devil.

2. Simplicity and Authenticity

We have seen how simplicity and authenticity were characteristics of Saint Macarius that allowed him to travel light to his heavenly homeland, without any burdens of a false image. Likewise, Anba Epiphanius lived according to this spirit of Saint Macarius. Once, some brethren asked him to take severe measures against another brother who had committed many sins. Anba Epiphanius refused, preferring to continue being patient. The brethren were very unhappy, but the abbot knew he was following in the footsteps of Saint Macarius. One day, after the refectory, a monk who understood the deep desire of Anba Epiphanius not to judge the brethren, and the effort he had to make to deal with the strictest brethren,

---

[18] *Alphabetical Collection*, Macarius 11 (*Alphabetical*: 183).

CHAPTER 4

brought a piece of paper to him that had an apothegm of Saint Macarius that says:

> Since Abba Macarius was benevolent[19] in his relations with all the brothers, some folk said to him: 'Why do you conduct yourself like this?' He said: 'I served my Lord for twelve years so he would grant me this spiritual gift; are you all advising me to set it aside?'[20]

Anba Epiphanius read it. Then he raised his head to the monk and said, smiling jokingly, "Where is it that you find these things?"

Father Matthew the Poor comments on this apothegm with:

> 'Simplicity' here means humility. The brethren who asked him the question are of the type who like to deify their leaders. The grace Macarius speaks of is the grace of a humble soul. At first glance, these words seem to us of little importance, concerning an event that is negligible. In reality, Saint Macarius deliberately reveals to us here the profound dimension of his life hidden with God. He admits that for twelve years he had not ceased praying and fighting with God and with himself to cross the abyss of a pretended sobriety, the abyss of the purported respect that belongs to authority, and the precipice of the ephemeral human glory that a lured monastic community projects on the superior. For this,

---

[19] The Greek text has *en akakía* which can also mean "with simplicity."

[20] *Alphabetical Collection*, Macarius 9 (*Alphabetical*: 182).

"THE SPIRIT OF SAINT MACARIUS"

he pleaded with God insistently that his life remain simple and humble in words and deeds so that he could spend all his monastic life as a beginner, with the same simplicity of spirit and the same humility, without making his monks perceive (and without the monks making him perceive) that he was better than others. From this story, it is evident how the scene of Macarius speaking with his spiritual children, the monks, aroused the sarcasm of some advanced monks who had fallen into the trap of the respect, the affected reverence, and the affected gravity of a superior that he who is advanced in years or rank imposes on those who are inferior to him. These are things that a sick community can impose on its superior or whoever presides. But from Macarius' resolute response, it is very clear that he was well aware of the smallness with which he lived, and that this smallness was susceptible to the blame and hilarity of these people who considered themselves great. The fact that he openly said that for twelve years he had prayed for himself to live in such a small and simple way confirms that he considered this behavior a model of life and the background against which he constantly moved. He had desired it, and God had given it to him as a charism.[21]

Anba Epiphanius the monk—and more so as the abbot—felt called to live concretely in the relationship with the brethren according to the verse, "If your eye is simple, your whole body will be luminous" (Matt.

---

[21] *Macarius*: 24-25.

6:22). In short, Anba Epiphanius was a man who lived simply. With a long and painful spiritual and human experience, he received from God the gift of continually re-creating and regenerating others, through love, in view of the Kingdom of Heaven. Anba Epiphanius' strength resided in his profound humanity. He was a monk in the true sense of the word because he did not lose his humanity. On the contrary, it was transfigured through his prayer, his asceticism, his faithful communing with the holy mysteries, his love, and his service towards everyone. His divinized humanity meant that he looked at all things and all people through the light of God that permeates everything, with that 'simple' eye of which Christ speaks. And it is in this way that he also saw all things, as "To the pure, all things are pure" (Tit. 1:15).

3. *Judge Not*

From this simplicity and purity, Anba Epiphanius also chose not to judge. We have already seen a concrete case that exemplified what not judging practically meant for him. Anba Epiphanius explained the importance of not judging in this way:

> Judgment and condemnation hide so many other sins within: jealousy, envy, hatred, chatter... To condemn

means to lack love. And if love is lacking, Christ is lacking.[22]

Even Macarius, like so many other Desert Fathers, has often insisted on Christ's commandment not to judge, "Judge not, and you shall not be judged. Condemn not, and you shall not be condemned. Forgive, and you will be forgiven" (Luke 6:37). Abba Paphnutius, a disciple of Saint Macarius, once said about his spiritual father:

> I besought my father [Macarius], saying, 'Tell me a saying!' but he said, 'Do no evil to anybody and do not condemn anybody. Keep these [commandments] and you are being saved.'[23]

"Not condemning" is therefore considered by Saint Macarius to be on the same level as "not to cause harm to anyone." For Macarius, judging is also linked to three other factors. First of all—as can be seen from the story with Saint Macarius of Alexandria, who expelled two brethren who sinned—one usually judges thinking he knows the whole truth. Most of the time, this is illusory. Hence, regarding the saying in question, Saint Macarius the Great reverses the condemnation issued by Saint Macarius of Alexandria and

---

[22] From the conference with the monks of Bose on May 26, 2016.

[23] *Alphabetical Collection*, Macarius 28 (*Alphabetical*: 187).

CHAPTER 4

expelled the latter in view of repentance, "because [Macarius the Great] loved him."[24]

Additionally, judging expresses a more or less hidden declaration of personal holiness: one considers oneself better than others.

Finally, judgement is often mixed with anger or resentment towards a given person. Saint Macarius warns that, even when a judgement may appear fair, it actually jeopardizes the salvation of those who judge, because it can hide the satisfaction of a sin:

> The same Abba Macarius said: 'If you are moved to anger in reproving somebody, you [merely] satisfy your own passion. Do not go lose your own self in order to save others.'[25]

4. Mercy: The Story of the Monk and the Jar

Great mercy characterized the abbacy of Anba Epiphanius. Once again, Anba Epiphanius was fully aware of the spirit that animated Saint Macarius, as well as himself. To a brother who once asked him to define Saint Macarius' monasticism in one word he replied, "Monasticism of mercy."

A famous saying, attributed in the Copto-Arabic collection *Bustān al-Ruhbān* precisely to Macarius, and which is worth reporting in full, illustrates the

---

[24] *Alphabetical Collection*, Macarius 21 (*Alphabetical*: 185).
[25] *Alphabetical Collection*, Macarius 17 (*Alphabetical*: 184).

"THE SPIRIT OF SAINT MACARIUS"

spirit with which Macarius lived his quality of 'father of monks':

> In a cell, there was a brother who had done a terrible thing. The news reached Father Macarius, who did not want to rebuke him. When the brethren found out, they started impatiently to spy on the brother until the woman entered his place. They told some brethren to continue spying on him while they went to tell Father Macarius. After reporting the fact to him, Saint Macarius said, 'Brethren, do not believe this story. This brother of ours cannot do such a thing!' To which they replied, 'Abba, come and see for yourself, so you will believe what we have told you.' The saint got up and went with them to the brother's cell as if he were going to greet him, and he commanded the brethren to move away from him a little. As soon as the brother realized that the Abba [Macarius] was coming, he became unsettled, and, trembling, he took the woman and hid her inside a large barrel that was at his place. When the Abba entered, he sat on the barrel and commanded the brethren to enter. When they entered, they inspected the cell but found no one. Unable to lift the saint from the barrel, they spoke with their brother, and then [Macarius] commanded them to leave. Once they left, the saint took the brother by his hand and said to him: 'My brother, judge yourself before you are judged [by God], because the judgement belongs to God.' Then he took his leave and left. As he went out, a voice came to him that said: 'Blessed are you, Macarius the Spiritual, who made yourself like your Creator so that you,

CHAPTER 4

like him, cover the faults of others.' Later on, the brother returned to himself and became a wise monk, a fighter, and a brave hero.[26]

Father Matthew the Poor comments on this passage comparing Saint Macarius' gesture to that of Christ with the sinful woman, recorded in the Gospel of John:

> In this passage, we are faced with the incredible and unparalleled spiritual beauty of Saint Macarius. It is as if we were, once again, in the presence of Christ himself and the sinful woman, witnessing those words full of extraordinary divine sweetness that were pronounced from the mouth of Christ, "Neither do I condemn you; go and sin no more." (John 8:11). Saint Macarius, here, brethren, has reached the summit of the Gospel. He put on the image of Christ, or rather, Christ Himself, and similarly replicated before us the episode of the sinful woman. Indeed, we can say that the two episodes can be superimposed in such an extraordinary way that they go beyond the capabilities of human nature. What amazes me here, in the story of the monk, the woman, and the barrel, is Macarius' extreme sensitivity towards what that monk caught in the very act must have felt. Brethren, it is impossible for a father according to the flesh or even a spiritual father to behave

---

[26] Apothegm n° 388 in *Bustān*: 184. A version with similar elements is attributed to abba Ammonas in the Greek alphabetical collection (Ammonas 10). But in the tradition of Scetis this Apothegm is *par excellence* of Saint Macarius the Great.

"THE SPIRIT OF SAINT MACARIUS"

in this same way. Such behavior comes only from those who have managed to love the human sinner's soul with a divine love, as Christ alone knows how to love her. Saint Macarius saw a naked soul, and for this reason he stripped himself of the habit of his role as a father and superior and covered this soul that all his brethren wanted to pillory. Macarius saw a dangerously wounded human soul that the brethren wanted to bleed to death by inflicting the coup de grace: the public scandal. Macarius thus placed himself in the middle, endangering his dignity, his justice, his fatherhood, and even his purity, to heal this wound under his protection and in his embrace. And the wound really healed, and that monk got up from his fall. It was as if God had covered him on account of Macarius' extraordinary delicacy. Macarius saw a wounded soul in the image of God rather than sin. Sin, despite its monstrosity, has failed to affect Macarius' extraordinary tenderness in relating to the human soul, even when the soul is in a terrible situation, as in this case.[27]

This image that the Copto-Arabic tradition conveys is just wonderful, "Once they left, the saint took the brother by his hand and said... 'My brother...'" Saint Macarius only cares about his brother's salvation. Neither sin, nor chatter, nor the risk of jeopardizing his figure as a superior before the most strict and zealous brethren occupies his thinking. He takes his brother by the hand to raise him up, like an *alter*

---

[27] *Macarius*: 26-27.

CHAPTER 4

Christus who descends into existential hell and takes the fallen Adam by the hand.

Father Matthew wrote about the superior's need to use mercy:

> When a brother came to me after doing something wrong, I was faced with two options: either I should have remained silent, showing him my love, loving him with that tenderness that is proper of divine love which covers all defects and a multitude of sins; or else I had to confront him with the truth, rebuking him and pointing out his mistake in order to correct him. I spent my whole life speaking the truth with my brethren, with the Church, with people, with the whole world. In doing so, I put love behind me. But only this year, I realized that I had come to a dangerous stage, to the extreme point at which the truth can reach, to a point after which I would throw up the experience of a lifetime. Love must prevail.[28]

These were not mere words. The abbot often recalled the gestures of mercy that Father Matthew practiced towards the brethren who made mistakes and were aware of their mistakes, especially if they

---

[28] Catechesis entitled *Al-Ḥaqq Wa-l-Maḥabba* (Truth and Love). The English translation has been published in full in Matthew the Poor, *Sojourners* (Wādī al-Naṭrūn: St Macarius Press, 2019): 225-237. This catechesis was pronounced by father Matthew the Poor in 1967 in Wādī al-Rayyān. At the monastery a stenographic transcript has been preserved by one of the monks who lived with Father Matthew.

"THE SPIRIT OF SAINT MACARIUS"

were grave mistakes. He recounted once that Father Matthew learned that a monk had once committed a serious sin, and he went to visit Father Matthew in the annex that the monastery has on the north coast. Anba Epiphanius was there at the time and saw the scene. He recounts:

> As soon as he saw him, Father Matthew ran towards him, saying: 'Father, how are you? How long we have not seen each other! I missed you very much. Come, let us have something to eat together.'[29]

Anba Epiphanius comments on this episode:

> Father Matthew the Poor taught us that the monks who make mistakes, even if they make serious mistakes, are those who need more love and welcoming. In order to repent and convert, they must feel that they are loved. Even if you know his mistake, try not to blame him but to treat him with mercy.[30]

Much could be written about the mercy of Bishop Epiphanius. I believe that during his years as a simple monk, he had so much internalized the episode of the barrel and the attitude of Father Matthew the Poor towards sinners that, when he was given the function of superior, he kept them as a polar star that guided him in the service to the brethren. In the monastery,

---

[29] From a private conversion with the editor on September 19, 2015.

[30] From the same conversion.

CHAPTER 4

the episodes in which Anba Epiphanius covered the sins of the monks are countless. Until the last moment of his life, if it was necessary to mention a sin or a flaw, he never mentioned the name of the monk who had committed the sin. He always just said, "A monk..." If the converser insisted on wanting to know the name, he used to reply, "It is not important."

It was known to all in the monastery that there were a number of monks who opposed him since the day of his appointment. These monks had created a WhatsApp group in which they continuously criticized him, often going well beyond the limits of good manners. When the monks close to him begged him to order the closure of this group, he simply replied, "I respect freedom of expression. It is through love, not by force, that we will earn them." Anba Epiphanius firmly believed in the patient love of which Saint Paul speaks (cf. 1 Cor. 13:4), so much so as to consider patience toward a sinful brother a form of love. Once, in 2015, a monk of the Monastery of Bose (Italy) asked him, "What is patience?" He explained:

> Patience is love. The Apostle says, in fact, that love is patient. God Himself has an abundance of patience with us because He loves us. It is very easy for me to expel those people who disturb, but then they will find themselves on the street. On the other hand, I hope that

"THE SPIRIT OF SAINT MACARIUS"

with patience and love, even if it takes ten years, they will repent.

Still, with regard to these disturbing elements, an elder once asked him to be stricter and to think seriously about expelling them. Anba Epiphanius' tone became serious and he said to him:

> I am a father, not a general manager. At night I do not sleep, thinking and praying for their salvation.

Anba Epiphanius was the 'man of the barrel,' the man of mercy, of forgiveness, of the love that generates and awaits, the faithful disciple of Saint Macarius and Father Matthew the Poor. Many of his spiritual children have testified to the love they felt before this spiritual bishop and father, who fought to the last breath to remain an authentic monk, faithful to his vocation. This love was of such purity, simplicity, and harmony that brings to mind the saying that all this will be the air we will breathe in the Kingdom of Heaven.

5. Monk 'in the Making'

Like Saint Macarius, Anba Epiphanius considered himself a monk 'in the making,' still on the way. We read in the Great Letter of Macarius:

> And even though before God they are honored, still they see themselves as unworthy, and though they progress spiritually, they see themselves as beginners, and

CHAPTER 4

though they are great, still they despise themselves and consider themselves nothing... Such souls will be able to please God and become heirs of the Kingdom. Having a contrite heart, being poor in spirit, always hungry, thirsty for justice, and longing for perfect honors, they will be rewarded with the highest gifts for their distinguished love towards God.[31]

There is another story about Saint Macarius that Anba Epiphanius was fond of. After being tempted for five years by the thought of going into the inner desert to see who lived there, Abba Macarius understood that the thought came from God. When he went to the inner desert, he found two naked monks who lived in total renunciation of the world and in deep asceticism. Saint Macarius was so impressed by the meeting with these two anchorites that, when he narrated the episode to the brethren, he introduced and ended the story with the phrase:

> I have not yet become a monk. I have however seen monks.[32]

Anba Epiphanius often repeated this phrase—especially when he met other monks—which indicated

---

[31] Macarius, *The Great Letter*, 5:2 (according to Staats). Cf. Werner Jaeger, *Two Rediscovered Works of Ancient Christian Literature: Gregory of Nyssa and Macarius* (Leiden: Brill, 1954): 255-256 (translation from the Greek).

[32] Apothegm n° 37 in *Bustān*: 28-29. Cf. *Alphabetical Collection*, Macarius 2 (*Alphabetical*: 178).

how he felt himself to be 'on the way.' How could a bishop like Anba Epiphanius, a father of monks and superior of one of the oldest monasteries in Christianity, say such a phrase? Considering that many saw him as a clear model of what it means to be a monk, these words only aroused all the more wonder.

6. Eschatological Man

The Bohairic life of Saint Macarius mentions:

> He was thinking to himself, as was his custom, about his passing away and his meeting God, and the judgment that would be passed against him at that time.[33]

Saint Macarius was all focused on the true homeland; the heavenly Jerusalem. This was the secret that guided his earthly life, and this was also the secret of Anba Epiphanius. He lived immersed in a 'daily eschatology.' His every thought, his every action, and his every desire was oriented towards the Lord who comes, towards the moment of the terrible and blessed encounter with the luminous face of the risen Christ. We heard him say more than once, "When I will see Him [Jesus Christ] face to face, what will I

---

[33] *Bohairic Life of Saint Macarius of Scetis*, 41:17. The paragraph numbers are taken from Satoshi Toda (ed.), *Vie de S. Macaire l'égyptien* (Piscataway, NJ: Gorgias Press, 2011). Cf. *Spiritbearer*: 192.

CHAPTER 4

say to Him?" These words were enough to convey a teaching and bring his spiritual children to their feet!

Father Matthew the Poor also lived this way. In one of Anba Epiphanius' homilies, he offered this eschatological tension with which Father Matthew lived to a crowd of faithful gathered for the tenth anniversary of his departure on June 10, 2016, which fell on the day after the Feast of Ascension. Anba Epiphanius, from the pulpit of the church of Saint Macarius, quoted a long passage from his spiritual father:

> The true monk is the one who continually lives the feast of Ascension, to whom what is above, the Spirit and the Truth, are enough all his days. On earth he fears nothing; neither tribulation, nor anguish, nor persecution, nor hunger, nor nakedness, nor danger, nor sword (cf. Rom. 8:35). On earth he desires nothing (cf. Ps. 73:25): neither honor, nor particular friendships, nor supremacy, nor power, nor praise, nor names, nor appearance, nor titles. Indeed, he mysteriously feeds on what is above: the food of Truth and the drink of love. All those who feed on these two things forget what belongs to this world; they forget their family, their homeland, and even themselves. Every person in Christ desires the life of the world to come, according to the words of the Creed. On the other hand, brethren, the monk is already living this, since he died in this passing world. Ascension is not only a feast for us monks. It is

our daily work towards this world. It is the only life that is left to us.[34]

It may seem insignificant, but part of his being immersed in Christ and in the Eighth Day inaugurated by His Resurrection, is the fact that Anba Epiphanius did not celebrate his birthday. To those who wished him well, he always replied with his typical kindness that, "monks do not celebrate birthdays." A monk once wished him a happy birthday, and his response was as follows:

> Thanks, but please do not do that again! I believe that, instead of celebrating the beginning of our existence in the flesh, it is more beautiful to celebrate the feast of our existence and of our being in Christ, a mystery that repeats itself every day and every moment, often without us noticing. How can we accept greetings and gifts for an earthly day when, in Christ, our life has risen beyond time and space?

7. Delicacy

One last trait of Anba Epiphanius was his delicacy. His feelings were so delicate that very often he was moved to tears. Once, during an informal conversation in his last trip to Australia, he was asked why he was moved. He replied:

---

[34] Matthew the Poor, "Ṣuʿūd Al-Masīḥ" [Christ's Ascension], in *Id.*, *Al-Qiyāma Wa-l-Ṣuʿūd* [Resurrection and Ascension] (Wādī al-Naṭrūn: Monastery of Saint Macarius 2000³): 380.

CHAPTER 4

What always moves me to tears is God's love. When I feel His love filling me or my environment, I cannot hold back tears. When the love of God moves me or when I see that someone has suffered injustice, I feel I am filled with the bowels of God's mercies.

This aspect of his life seems inspired—yet again!—by a beautiful story attributed to Saint Macarius:

> Abba Peter used to say of the holy Macarius that one day he came across an anchorite and found him distressed. He asked him what he would like to eat, for there was nothing in the cell. When he said, 'A cookie,' the strong man did not hesitate to get himself to the city of Alexandria and give [it] to the brother. The wonder became known to nobody.[35]

Two preliminary notes are worthy of this saying. First and foremost, the episode was certainly wonderful and extraordinary—the Abba of the desert, the father of Scetis, goes to Alexandria to bring a cookie for a hermit, or rather *the* cookie that he liked! Furthermore, the saying defines Saint Macarius, for the simple fact of having made that gesture, as "the strong man." We prefer to translate the Greek word *andreíos*, which literally means 'manly,' as 'strong', instead of 'courageous,' although the latter is also correct. The reason is that we see that Saint Macarius is called 'manly' in the sense of being 'strong in love.' Being

---

[35] *Alphabetical Collection*, Macarius 8 (*Alphabetical*: 182).

"THE SPIRIT OF SAINT MACARIUS"

'manly', in Christianity, has nothing to do with 'masculinity' or the courage of a certain mythology. On the contrary 'manly' means being the human being that God wanted us to be, that is 'perfect in love.' Thus, Saint Macarius was in possession of a love so great as to push him to make about a day's trip to please his brother. The purpose seems obvious; Saint Macarius loved others and cared for their joy. He did not miss the opportunity to make his distressed brother rejoice—he, Macarius, who, when offered a glass of wine, deprived himself of water for a whole day![36]

Secondly, the fact that this episode "became known to nobody" is, of course, less obvious since the whole world now knows it! Perhaps it is necessary to read between the lines and understand that Saint Macarius made other similar gestures of which, however, we know nothing.

---

[36] "They used to say of Abba Macarius that, if he was enjoying the company of some brothers, he would impose a rule on himself: 'If there is wine, drink for the brothers' sake and in place of one cup of wine don't drink water for one day'. The brothers would give him wine by way of refreshment and the elder would take it with pleasure in order to torture himself. But his disciple, aware of [his] practise, said to the brothers: 'For the Lord's sake, do not give it to him for otherwise he is going to afflict himself in his cell'. When the brothers learnt [this] they did not give him [wine] any more" (*Alphabetical Collection*, Macarius 10; Cf. Alphabetical: 182-83).

CHAPTER 4

Anba Epiphanius had the same delicacy as Saint Macarius. The strong love of God that inhabited his heart caused him to try not to miss an opportunity to give joy to the brethren with small gestures.

Once, he was leaving for an ecclesial commitment abroad. He called a brother to tell him and then said, "Do you need anything from there?" The brother, embarrassed that the abbot was so interested in him, responded timidly, "But father, leave the matter; do not tire yourself for me. Your Grace will have so many things to do that I am the last thing to think about!" Anba Epiphanius insisted, "Do not worry! Just tell me what I can bring you." To this, the brother replied, "Father, if you really don't mind, there is a type of coffee they have there. It does not cost much, and you find it in supermarkets, so you don't have to waste time going around." The brother did not know it was possible to buy it in Egypt. Anba Epiphanius burst out laughing, perhaps because he expected something much more complicated and cumbersome than a pack of coffee. "Do you mean that coffee? Just that?" Embarrassed by the laughter that apparently seemed to diminish the request, the monk replied with embarrassment, "Yes, but only if it is possible." Anba Epiphanius replied that he would do everything possible to bring that coffee, greeted him, and hung up. Two hours later, someone knocked on the door of the monk's cell. The latter

"THE SPIRIT OF SAINT MACARIUS"

opened and found no one. There was only a bag hanging from the handle. Inside, he found the coffee he had asked for and in large quantities.

CHAPTER 5
TEACHINGS
ON WHICH HE INSISTED

As we have seen, Anba Epiphanius was a faithful disciple of the Desert Fathers and of Father Matthew the Poor. He devoted a good part of his scientific and spiritual activities to the former. The edition of the *Bustān al-Ruhbān*, the Copto-Arabic collection of the apothegms of the Desert Fathers, which he completed in 2013 after years of work, caused him to be totally immersed in desert spirituality allowing him to memorize a substantial number of sayings. He considered the tradition of apothegms to be the most important source of monastic teaching, especially of the Scetis tradition. Whenever it was necessary to meditate on a monastic theme, the first texts to which Anba Epiphanius had recourse were always represented by the collections of the apothegms. Only after reading them did he turn to secondary literature. This allowed him to better observe the issues because, for him, it was like standing on the shoulders of giants, who had already faced all the primary problems related to monastic life. The sayings of the fathers tell us about monks with their strengths and weaknesses, with their successes and failures. And this is what

CHAPTER 5

encourages today's monastics to persevere in their spiritual struggle.

In a passage that was intended to be published in the introduction to the edition of the *Bustān al-Ruhbān* edited by Anba Epiphanius, he wrote:

> The lives and sayings of the Desert Fathers paint a real image of a life lived, rich in victories, indeed, but in which there is no lack of failures. If we are faced with high levels of spirituality and mortification of the ego, it is because the monk has totally submitted to the work of grace in his heart, remaining alert, watching, and fighting for long years. If, however, we are faced with stories that tell of falls and sins, it is because the monk is a man who fights in an arena and, during the fight, can be injured and even killed. But in the end, he will still receive the crown, provided that he does not throw in the towel and does not abandon his hope in the Lord Jesus.[1]

It is therefore impossible to fully understand the monastic teaching of Anba Epiphanius without having read at least one or more collections of the apothegms.

Secondly, it is equally impossible to penetrate the monastic vision of our abbot without knowing the monastic heritage of Father Matthew.[2] Anba

---

[1] Taken from the recording of a conference delivered by Anba Epiphanius to the monks at the Monastery of Saint Macarius on January 12, 2014.

[2] On general monastic teachings of Father Matthew, see

TEACHINGS ON WHICH HE INSISTED

Epiphanius elaborates on many of the ideas addressed by Father Matthew in an original way and insists on some others that he considered most urgent in his time. It is good to remember that the era in which Father Matthew wrote about monasticism can be considered a period that focused on monasticism without other motives, and in which the sense of community was very strong. Those who did not feel called to this type of monasticism sought other ways; transferring to other monasteries, going to serve in the world as priests, or returning to the world as laymen.

Anba Epiphanius, on the contrary, experienced an era of great upheavals in which the monastic vision of the Monastery of Saint Macarius was about to be swept away. Becoming a bishop, therefore, he tried to cure these wounds, the main one of which was the loss of the sense of communion with a consequent 'monastic individualism,' which he considered to be dangerous.

It is with this mindset that Anba Epiphanius insisted on teachings that would resist such contenders to the true monastic life.

Matthew the Poor, *Sojourners: Monastic Letters and Spiritual Teachings from the Desert* (Wādī al-Naṭrūn: St Macarius Press, 2019).

CHAPTER 5

1. Who is the Monk?

For Anba Epiphanius, the monk is a person who, having abandoned the world—his family, his profession, and the vanity of the world—intensely seeks to live a relationship of love with Christ, being united in Him through continuous prayer, Eucharist, meditation on Scripture, work, asceticism, and service to the brethren. A member's entry into the monastery entails rite of passage similar to a funeral ritual, symbolic of the monastic's death to the world and rising to a new life with Christ, even being given a new first and last name.[3]

He constantly tries to live a life of repentance as a sojourner and pilgrim on earth (cf. Heb. 11:13), keeping his gaze fixed on the heavenly Jerusalem (cf. Luke 9:51).[4] By constantly raising himself towards God, he brings with him the whole of humanity with which he is intimately united, even though he has separated himself from everyone.

---

[3] Each monk receives a new name from the abbot at the moment of ordination, and assumes, as a surname, the monastery he belongs to. All the monks of Saint Macarius have as surname al-Maqārī, that is 'the Macarian.'

[4] It is interesting that in the Coptic Church the pericope Luke 9:51-62 is read, among other occasions, on the eve of the Feast of Ascension. In the exegesis that the Church makes of it, Christ prepares to ascend towards the true Jerusalem, the heavenly one, from which He descended.

TEACHINGS ON WHICH HE INSISTED

A monk cannot live his vocation without creating an intimate relationship with Christ. Without it, the monk is doomed to be lost. Anba Epiphanius wrote:

> God's first words to Abraham, father of the patriarchs, were 'Get out of your country and from your family' (Gen. 12:1). Following this example, Saint Anthony left his home and kinship. He left the company of friends, family ties, and neighborly and worldly relationships to totally devote himself to a personal relationship with the Lord Jesus... Leaving one's own land and kinship does not imply any kind of contempt for others... Here what is meant is the abandonment of all those relationships that lead the monk back to take an interest in the world and distance him from his only (pre)occupation, [5] or from his personal relationship with the Lord Jesus Christ.[6]

"The monk," he once said to a brother who asked him, "is the one who forgets himself in order to unite with Christ. We must forget ourselves to seek union with the Other."[7] The fuel of the monk which allows him to walk, or rather to run, the monastic way is the

---

[5] In Arabic *Hammuhu al-Waḥīd*. It is not easy to render in English. The term brings with it concern, care, promptness, occupation, interest, importance, intention, purpose, fixed idea.

[6] Anba Epiphanius, "Uḫruğ Min 'Ašīratika" [Get out of your family], *Al-Kirāza* (Official Magazine of the Coptic Orthodox Patriarchate), year 46, n° 3-4, January 26, 2018: 14.

[7] Cf. Anba Epiphanius, *So Great a Salvation* (Wādī al-Naṭrūn: St Macarius Press, 2020): 294.

CHAPTER 5

love of God for him, which allows the monk to love God and the brethren in turn:

> The most dangerous thing is to enter the monastery without love and not try to grow this virtue. It is love that will tell me how to behave in any situation, with my brethren, with my father confessor, and with the workers of the monastery. It is love that governs all my behaviors and, obviously, also my relationship with the Lord.[8]

The asceticism of the monk is therefore subordinated to this love and this union with God. It does not represent the goal of a monk's actions, but rather it is an important instrument through which the flame of divine love stays alight. Not only asceticism, but everything the monk does must have this union with Christ as the cause and end, including prayer, work, fasting, and service to the brethren. The monk's ultimate goal is to prepare for death and the encounter with the One who loved him and Whom he loved all his life.

To a novice who asked him to summarize monasticism in a few words, Anba Epiphanius replied:

> Monasticism is the easiest way to unite with God. Do you remember Seraphim of Sarov and his dialogue

---

[8] From a monastic conference held on April 15, 2015 in the presence of newly consecrated monks on Saturday of Light (Holy Saturday), April 11, 2015, in the novice hall in the Monastery of Saint Macarius.

TEACHINGS ON WHICH HE INSISTED

with Motovilov?[9] The monk who takes his path seriously manages to experience things similar to those experienced by Seraphim. He experiences the strength and sweetness of the Holy Spirit. Indeed, even in the world there is holiness, and in the world, there are great saints. But for me, monasticism represents a more leveled path to holiness. In the monastery, everything helps the monk unite with God. This union with God can be made explicit even after a year in the novitiate. Or, there are people who have lived in the monastery for fifty years and have never experienced or felt it. What matters is that we must be very focused on the purpose for which we made ourselves monks and leave the rest in the hands of the Lord.

As one of the apothegms of Saint Macarius goes:

People's wills differ, so that a person with an active and fervent will can advance in one hour in a way that no one else can advance in fifty years if their will is slack.[10]

In following this path, the monk must arm himself with patience and endurance to face the war of demons and passions that materializes above all in the form of thoughts and doubts, in particular regarding

---

[9] Saint Seraphim of Sarov (1754-1833) became well known in Egypt starting from the mid-twentieth century. His biography, his dialogue with Motovilov, and his sayings have influenced Coptic contemporary spirituality. You can read the dialogue with Motovilov here: https://pravoslavie.ru/47866.html (accessed: July 2023).

[10] Apothegm n° 51 in *Bustān*, 38.

CHAPTER 5

brotherly love, injustice, insult, contempt, and daily temptations. This is why, to define the monk, Anba Epiphanius used an apothegm that tells of the encounter between Moses the Black and Zacharias:

> ...Zacharias, taking his hood, put it under his feet and crushed it. Then he picked it up and put it back on his head saying, 'If the monk does not become so crushed[11] he will not be saved.'[12]

This acceptance of being crushed indicates, on the one hand, the acceptance of the wounds of the daily struggle that the monk must face. On the other hand, Anba Epiphanius read this being crushed as the daily effort of obedience, which means giving up one's will to accept that of another, even when it appears to be less suitable or even wrong. In concrete terms, it means, above all, enduring the fact that one's thoughts and opinions, even if right, might be ignored, derided, and despised. Either way, whether to accept being wounded in battle or to obey, being crushed means accepting to die to oneself. It is then that the monk's salvation begins.[13]

---

[11] In Arabic the term *munsaḥiq*, used here, can mean 'crushed,' 'smashed' but also 'contrite.'

[12] Apothegm n° 196 in *Bustān*: 101.

[13] In the monastic spirituality of the desert, the term 'salvation,' means the eschatological salvation, in view of which a person becomes a monk. But it also means the success, with the help of God, in the spiritual struggle against the passions and one's 'own will' that inhabit the monk, through self-mortification in

TEACHINGS ON WHICH HE INSISTED

Once, he met a young man who was about to join the monastery. He asked him, "How old are you?" The young man replied, "Thirty." Anba Epiphanius continued, "Brother, monks live long! Do not look at the past thirty years, but think about the many you have left to live! Do you think you can live this life for the next fifty years?" Seeing the young man's determination, Anba Epiphanius tried to encourage him, saying, "As Saint Macarius said, 'The well is deep, but the water is good and sweet.'[14] It is a difficult path, brother, but its joys are many."

One last element that Anba Epiphanius insisted on was that there is no half monk:

> In these years, I have noticed that in the monastic life, there is only one way, not two: either you are a monk, or you are nothing. And it is impossible to be both.[15]

This does not mean, of course, that the monk who is not a monk cannot transform and become one. At the same time, it does not mean that he who lives seriously does not have moments of fall,

---

order to live in God. When therefore one hears in the desert, "think about your salvation," this is not an invitation to spiritual selfishness, as it might seem. It means, on the one hand, "think about your personal struggles" (and it is implied, "do not judge others"), and on the other hand, "think about the ultimate goal of your becoming a monk" (i.e., the eschatological salvation).

[14] Cf. Apothegm n° 200 in *Bustān*: 102.

[15] From a monastic conference with the novices of the Monastery of Bose (Italy), September 10, 2015.

CHAPTER 5

discouragement, doubt, or laxity. What Anba Epiphanius is likely referring to is that it is easy to completely lose one's way and return to the world while living in a monastery. This is why the monastic struggle is based not only on the love of God but also on clarity of purpose.

2. *Clarity of Purpose*

A few days before their ordination, Anba Epiphanius reminded some novices of the importance of having the purpose of their 'exit' from the world clear. In doing so, he cited the story of Abba Arsenius the Great, who identified the key to proceeding in the monastic way by remembering the purpose for which the monk chose to enter the monastery:

> This is the word the elder used to repeat, 'Why did you get out [of the world], Arsenius?'[16]

Judging by the sayings, Abba Arsenius, finding himself doubting his salvation in a place as sinful and full of vanity as the court of Constantinople could be, sought the way of salvation and the possibility of not sinning.[17] If the initial drive—to seek peace in God by avoiding court vanity—was so strong as to bring him to the harsh Egyptian desert, no less strong was the

---

[16] *Alphabetical Collection*, Arsenius 40 (trans. from Greek).
[17] Cf. *Alphabetical Collection*, Arsenius 1 and 2 (cf. *Alphabetical*: 31-32).

TEACHINGS ON WHICH HE INSISTED

final goal for which Arsenius struggled as a monk. In fact, in a saying, we read:

> When he was about to give up the ghost, the brothers saw him weeping and they said to him, 'Are you too truly afraid, father?' He said to them, 'Truly, the fear that is with me in this hour has been with me ever since I became a monk,' and so he fell asleep.[18]

Therefore, the 'clarity of purpose' can indicate at the same time the motivation behind the choice to join the monastery—which can have its positive drive (to be saved) and its negative one (to move away from a place of perdition such as the court)—but also the final goal for which monastic life is lived.

Anba Epiphanius gave great importance to the 'purpose or reason why one gets out of the world' and considered it the second fuel that the monk can draw on to persevere in the monastic life, after the love of God. It is better for him not to undertake the monastic path at all if the goal is not 'correct.' An incorrect purpose, for him, indicated that one has left the world for substantially negative reasons (financial problems, bad family relationships, the impossibility of getting married, etc.) or for a desire that seeks something other than the Lord, such as the desire to become a priest, bishop, to do apostolate, to show off, to collect money etc. instead of a daily life of prayer, work, and

---

[18] *Alphabetical Collection*, Arsenius 40 (*Alphabetical*: 51).

CHAPTER 5

communion. The two aspects, negative drive and secondary ends, can inherently coexist.

The monk's horizon, for Anba Epiphanius, must be 'monasticism per se,' not in the sense of a solipsistic spiritual exercise in which monasticism itself becomes the purpose of life, since the center of monasticism remains Christ, but in the sense of not looking elsewhere for alternative ways. This means rejecting the great temptation of power in whatever form it may present itself, accepting to live in the cloistered space in a daily struggle through which the monk can grow in the love of God and in that of the brethren, constantly practicing the death of the ego. It takes little time to understand if the push at the base of the 'Abrahamic Exodus' possesses these requirements of clarity and purity. If the 'exodus' is 'inauthentic,' the monk gradually begins to no longer respect his rule of prayer, no longer does his monastic duty, no longer works, etc.

In other words, what is meant by 'righteous purpose'? Anba Epiphanius loved to resort to the image of the hare and the dogs that appears in a famous apothegm:

> Abba Hilarion was asked, 'How can it be right for a strenuous brother not to be offended when he seeth other monks returning to the world?' The old man said, 'It is meet that he should consider the hunting dogs which follow after hares, for as one of these dogs giveth

TEACHINGS ON WHICH HE INSISTED

chase to the hare so soon as he seeth it (now the other dogs which are his companions look at that dog as he runneth, and although they run with him for a certain time, they at length become exhausted and turn back, whilst he continueth his running by himself, and is not impeded in his headlong course, and he striveth to advance, and neither resteth nor ceaseth from running because of those who have remained behind, but he runneth until he hath overtaken that which he seeth, even as I have already said, and he feareth neither the stones which come in his way, nor the thorny brambles and briars, and passeth on among the thorns, and though often torn and lacerated thereby he neither resteth nor ceaseth from his course), so also for the brother, who wisheth to follow after the love of Christ, is it right to fasten his gaze upon the Cross until he overtaketh Him that was crucified, even though he see others who have begun to turn back.'[19]

Only the dog that has really seen the hare can run to the end to grab the hare, and is not interested in the injuries he suffers from running. Anba Epiphanius made this exegesis: the monk who did not find the precious Pearl, Christ, who did not feel his heart beat for Him, who in his life did not have a strong experience of grace, who did not at least glimpse the glory, peace, and joy of the Kingdom of heaven, who is not willing to bet his entire existence on eternal life,

---

[19] Cf. *Paradise*, book 2, saying n° 212: 199. Cf. also the abbreviated version in *Systematic*, 7:42 (*Systematic*: 114).

will hardly continue to run in the present.[20] The 'exodus,' therefore, which one must remember is not only the exodus out of the world, but also the exodus out of the flesh, that is, the moment of the passage to the afterlife.

Anba Epiphanius wrote to a monk:

Those who have a righteous purpose distinguish themselves from those who do not have it by how they consider 'the way that leads to the Kingdom' [i.e., monasticism]: for the first, who respects it, monasticism is a holy, joyful, and easy way; for the second, who despises it, it is very difficult and extremely boring.[21]

3. The Obstacle of Priesthood

Anba Epiphanius was convinced that what held monasticism back in the Coptic Church was the introduction of priesthood into monasteries. It is not the priesthood itself that is wrong, but rather its deviant correlation with monasticism. Although there is no room here to explain the relatively recent reasons and stages of this evolution (or rather involution) of Coptic monasticism, the result, however, is for Anba Epiphanius entirely negative.

First, early monasticism did not know the priesthood in this form. Saint Anthony and Saint

---

[20] From a personal conversation with the editor.
[21] From a personal correspondence with the editor, April 21, 2016.

TEACHINGS ON WHICH HE INSISTED

Pachomius were not priests, and we have no echo that Macarius, despite being a presbyter, ever celebrated when he became the spiritual father of Scetis.[22] For many years in Scetis, there was only one main monk-priest for a community that included thousands of monks. In the fourth and fifth centuries, the main priests were Abbas Isidore, Paphnutius, John Kolobós, and Daniel.[23] Father Matthew the Poor, who advocated monasticism without priesthood all his life, renounced to celebrate, even though he was a *qummuṣ*.[24]

Furthermore, for Anba Epiphanius, monasticism and priesthood are two substantially conflicting vocations because, if monasticism is based entirely on

---

[22] His biography seems to indicate that before Macarius went to live in the Desert of Scetis, he celebrated the Divine Liturgy alone in his cell. "Later, then, on an appointed day when he would receive the holy mysteries alone in his cell, as was his custom, and when he would stand at the altar as was his custom, he looked toward his right and suddenly saw there a cherub... the cherub said to him:... complete the service you have begun that has been entrusted to you and receive the holy mysteries" (*Spirit-bearer*: 68-69).

[23] These main presbyters were probably joined by an unspecified number of 'clerics' (cf. *Alphabetical Collection*, Moses 5) composed of both other assisting priests or deacons. In any case, the total number of priests who celebrated the Eucharist corresponded to the bare minimum and were a minority compared to the community at large.

[24] See note 3, p. 43.

CHAPTER 5

the acquisition of humility, the priesthood gives this voluntary lowering an upward, contrary force. The priest feels like a father and a guide and therefore claims to preside over the community liturgy and to celebrate special liturgies for guests who come to the monastery. Thus, the monk-priest risks abandoning the path of self-denial and instead seeks worldly recognition. In this sense, Anba Epiphanius made the ancient fear of Pachomius his own:

> He had deliberated on the subject and often told them that it was good not to ask for rank and honor, especially in a community, for fear this should be an occasion for strife, envy, jealousy, and then schisms to arise in a large community of monks. He told them, 'In the same way as a spark of fire, however small at the beginning, if cast into a threshing floor and not quickly quenched, destroys the year's labor, so the clerical dignity is the beginning of a temptation to love of power.'[25]

The other problem related to the monastic priesthood is that it arouses jealousy among monks. These jealousies are often so strong that the abbots are forced to ordain all the monks in their communities. Some monks show impatience at becoming priests,

---

[25] *First Greek Life of Pachomius*, 27. Cf. Armand Veilleux (ed.), *Pachomian Koinonia*, vol. I (Kalamazoo, MI: Cistercian Publications, 1980): 314. John Cassian inserts this discourse in the chapter on "vainglory" (Cf. *Id., Institutes*, 11.14).

and this creates strong tensions. In the community, therefore, an element of inequality insinuates itself that prevents the monks from all being brethren on equal terms, without discrimination or differences between one another.

According to Anba Epiphanius, another injury caused by the monastic priesthood is the threat to Eucharistic communion amongst the monastic order. The monk-priests celebrate liturgies parallel to the community ones (alone or with their guests), thus weakening the unifying force of the one weekly community Eucharistic liturgy. Thus, rather than acting as a unifier, as it is in its nature, the celebration of the liturgy separates.

For Anba Epiphanius, it was obviously impossible to completely do without monk-priests. It was necessary to order only the minimum number of monks necessary for the needs of the community and for generational change. He ordained six monks as priests in 2014.

*4. The Importance of Communion:
Church and Refectory*

Communion was near and dear to Anba Epiphanius' heart. At the time of Father Matthew, the community was cohesive thanks to the charismatic strength of its spiritual father, who was able to magnetize the brethren around him and who represented

CHAPTER 5

the center that held them together. When Father Matthew rested in the Lord, the community gradually fragmented, losing that initial centripetal force. This is why Anba Epiphanius insisted, on the one hand, on the one community liturgy in which everyone was invited to participate in and, on the other, on the unifying function of the agape fraternal meal in the refectory. For him, as for the tradition of Scetis, the refectory represents an extension of the ecclesial space, which is why the refectory is oriented to the east, like the churches, and one enters the space in silence, keeping the same spirit of prayer that one has in church. Just as in church, there should also be no discussion of worldly things. For Anba Epiphanius, the food consumed in the refectory represents an integral part of the Eucharistic mystery since it is 'sanctified food' on which a prayer of thanksgiving is recited. After all, Christ instituted the Eucharist in the context of a meal.

The unifying force of the refectory is a double communion. On the one hand, with the mouth, one shares a single meal on which it has been collectively prayed.[26] On the other hand, with the ears and the

---

[26] Before consuming the agape, the monks normally pray the ninth hour together as it has always been the custom in Scetis. In the absence of the abbot, one of the monk-priests then gives a long blessing which is followed by Our Father recited communally. At the end of the meal there is the final blessing on the

heart, one shares a single word, the sayings of the Desert Fathers, which constantly brings the monks back to the spirit of the origins.

Very often, coming out of the refectory, Anba Epiphanius used to say to the monk in charge of the kitchen, "*Leh aklak ma'assil kida?*" (How come the food that you cook tastes so good?)" or, "I am invited to eat in so many different places because of my responsibility as a bishop, but the food in the refectory is always sweeter in my mouth!" Anba Epiphanius was so convinced that the food eaten in communion had another flavor that in the refectory, he ate things he normally did not like.

5. *The Importance of the Spiritual Father and Discernment*

Coptic monasticism has no monastic rules on which to rely. When the monks of Saint Macarius asked Father Matthew the Poor, "What is our rule?," he replied, "There is no rule in Coptic monasticism. Our only rule is love." Therefore, in Coptic monasticism, there is great freedom that is unthinkable in Western monastic orders. But where does Father Matthew the Poor draw the link between freedom and love? No doubt this is from the Epistle to the Galatians, since the freedom of which Father Matthew

---

leftovers.

CHAPTER 5

speaks is evangelic freedom, "For freedom did Christ set us free" (Gal. 5:1 ASV). We have been called to freedom, but this freedom must not become an occasion for the flesh; rather, it must be an occasion to love more and, through love, serve one another (cf. Gal 5:13).

This freedom does not mean that the monk should not have a guide either. Two things are difficult for the monk to discern; the inspiration of the Holy Spirit, and personal illusions. "Here," says Father Wadid el Macari, "the importance of the spiritual father emerges in training one's disciple to acquire discernment and the ability to sift through [his thoughts]."[27]

With his spiritual father, the monk can fully experience this Christian freedom by avoiding slipping. The task of the spiritual father is to adapt the monastic life to each monk, properly portioning fasting, praying, work, etc. Anba Epiphanius wrote about the great importance of the relationship between the spiritual father and discernment:

> Discernment enables the spiritual father to teach his brethren how to understand and act in the best way in the face of the trials to which they are subjected. This implies that the spiritual father is called, through discernment, to indicate to the brethren any harmful or erroneous modes of action... There is no doubt that discernment implies the ability of the spiritual father to

---

[27] *Wadid*: 123.

discern the spiritual potential of people and the way in which to relate, in the most appropriate way, to the temptations to which they are subjected... In giving direction, it is dangerous that the spiritual father generalizes it. On the contrary, he must make use of discernment in dealing with the different needs and potentials of his disciples.[28]

The relationship between freedom and love emerges again when we speak of our spiritual father. For Anba Epiphanius, it was necessary that the spiritual father be capable of great love for his children so that they could fully live in the freedom of the Spirit.

6. *The Greatest of All Teachings*

Finally, we would like to emphasize the greatest teaching of Anba Epiphanius, which encompasses all the others: his consistency. There was no contradiction between what he said and taught versus his life, which made his teachings effective. Palladius' ancient collection of stories from the Egyptian desert, *Lausiac History*, asserts:

> Teaching does not consist in the harmony of words and syllables—sometimes men possess these who are as vile as can be—but in meritorious acts of character, cheerfulness, intrepidity, bravery, good temper; add to these,

---

[28] Epiphanius di San Macario, "Il discernimento nei Padri del deserto", in Filofej Artjušin et al., *Discernimento e vita cristiana* (Magnano: Qiqajon, 2019): 93-95.

CHAPTER 5

unfailing boldness, which generates words like a flame of fire. For if this had not been so, the great Teacher would not have said to His disciples, 'Learn from me, for I am meek and lowly in heart' (Matt. 11:29).[29]

Because of Anba Epiphanius' consistency, his detractors also respected him. This consistency allowed the Abbot Epiphanius to teach by osmosis. There was no need for numerous words; he 'infected' his disciples with his spiritual beauty. "It was enough to look at him," to paraphrase a saying of the Desert Fathers.[30] This is the strength of the saints, which is derived from Christ Himself. As the Scripture says, "Of them the world was not worthy" (Heb. 11:38). Indeed, we were not worthy of this meek man, of this *kalógeros*, this "beautiful elder," a title that is applied in the monastic writings to those elders who have particularly radiated the pure beauty of the Spirit.

---

[29] Palladius, *Lausiac History* (New York: Macmillan Company, 1918): 38-39.
[30] Cf. Apothegm n°29 in *Bustān*: 23-24. *Alphabetical Collection*, Anthony 27 (*Alphabetical*: 37).

CHAPTER 6
ANBA EPIPHANIUS'
UNIVERSE

1. His Academic Interests

Anba Epiphanius has exerted considerable academic and ecclesiastical effort in many areas, first and foremost in the tradition of the Desert Fathers, which he loved deeply. In the first years of his entry into the monastery, he digitally transcribed the four books of the Arabic collection of the Ascetical Homilies of Saint Isaac of Nineveh and then the text of *Bustān al-Ruhbān*. As the monks of old were required to practice the art of *nisāḥa*[1]—as one of the possible forms of *melétē*[2]—Anba Epiphanius strived to 'modernize' the

---

[1] The art of *nisāḥa* consists in copying by hand, in one's cell, texts of the Scriptures, or the Church Fathers, or the monastic Fathers, as a spiritual exercise rather than a literary work. In particular, in Egypt, an author who was often copied was Saint Isaac the Syrian (or Isaac of Nineveh, 7th century) who is still considered one of the great monastic masters of Egyptian monasticism. Over the centuries, this practice has also given rise to some splendidly illustrated handwritten masterpieces.

[2] *Melétē* (in Arabic *haḏīḏ*) does not refer to something analogous to 'meditation' in the modern sense of the word. It is rather a constant repetition or rumination, in a low voice or, less

CHAPTER 6

monastic practice of *nisāḥa*, and this had a great impact on his spiritual life.

The scientific edition of *Bustān al-Ruhbān* is certainly his most important effort in this area. This work allowed him to live in the company of the Desert Fathers for long days, indeed for years. By virtue of frequenting them, he was, so to speak, 'infected' by them and ended up resembling them in his love for solitude and silence, the great inner peace that radiated around him, his personal asceticism and the minimalism of his cell, his humility and refusal of any honor, his abnegation, taking charge of the mistakes of others and refraining from answering back the offenses he received except with greater love and goodness. In the spirituality of the Desert Fathers, he had found the pearl of great value that quickly leads to the Kingdom and union with Christ. Yet, the long years of work on *Bustān al-Ruhbān* have also benefited many readers and scholars.

Anba Epiphanius carried out the examination and comparison of the text of the apothegms of six manuscripts of the *Bustān* present in the monastery, of

---

commonly, in silence, of some verses of Scripture learned by heart, or of a short form of a prayer inspired by the Scripture, or the practice of the so-called 'Jesus Prayer' which originated in the Egyptian wilderness and in Scetis specifically. The art of *nisāḥa* was considered a form of *melétē*.

which the oldest is *Siyar* 7 (373)[3] from the 18th century. For the first time, Anba Epiphanius identified the sayings, numbered them, and established the correspondence between each saying and the other numerous collections of apothegms and monastic hagiographic texts preserved in various ancient languages. This part of the job is the one that took him the most time. It is difficult to estimate how much time he devoted to studying the various collections, some of which occupy numerous volumes.

Another field of interest, of which he was no less fond, was the study of ancient liturgies. As a young monk, he dealt with finding the original Greek text of the three anaphoras still in use in the Coptic Church (those of Saint Basil, Saint Gregory, and Saint Mark/Saint Cyril). He was fascinated by the flavor that these texts offer in their original language, making us relive the time of the Fathers. In this context, he published the Greek text of the anaphoras, accompanied by an accurate scientific introduction and an annotated Arabic translation. For the last of these anaphoras (that of Saint Mark/Saint Cyril), he was not satisfied with offering the Greek text and its Arabic translation, but he studied all the primitive forms that have come down to us in the oldest manuscripts (such

---

[3] Numbering according to the inventory of Father Ugo Zanetti (*Les manuscrits de Dair Abu Maqar: inventaire* (Patrick Cramer: Geneva, 1986): 54).

CHAPTER 6

as those of Strasbourg, Dayr al-Balāyza, Barcelona, and others).[4] In 2017, Anba Epiphanius republished the Greek text of the three anaphoras with a rich philological introduction and an annotated Arabic translation focusing on one particular codex, the *Kacmarcik codex*, copied at the Monastery of Saint Anthony the Great in AD 1345. The importance of this manuscript is particularly linked to the anaphora of Saint Mark/Saint Cyril as it is the only codex to contain the complete Greek text of this anaphora currently used in the Coptic Church, a text that differs in many points from the text used in the Byzantine Church.

Another major subject that attracted his attention was the Great Euchology of the White Monastery, already published in the original Sahidic Coptic and in French by Father Emmanuel Lanne.[5] In this euchology, Anba Epiphanius discovered numerous

---

[4] On these ancient Alexandrian liturgies see Ronald Jasper and Geoffrey J. Cuming. *Prayers of the Eucharist: Early and Reformed* (Collegeville, MN: Liturgical Press, 2019): 52–54, 79–81.

[5] Emmanuel Lanne, *Le Grand euchologe du Monastère blanc* (Paris: Firmin-Didot, 1958). Emmanuel Lanne (1923-2010) was a worldly renown theologian and coptologist, a foremost expert on the Christian East, most active at the Second Vatican Council, where he collaborated in drawing up various decrees, an eminent protagonist of theological and ecumenical dialogue, to which he made a fundamental contribution at the highest international level. He was a close friend of the Monastery of Saint Macarius.

ancient anaphoras that were part of the liturgical heritage of the Coptic Church and have been lost, such as that of Saint Matthew, Saint Thomas, Saint Timothy the Patriarch of Alexandria, and others. He published the contents of this euchology, in the original Sahidic Coptic and in the Arabic translation, in eleven articles that appeared in the journal of *Alexandria School* from 2010 to 2013, and in 2014 he collected all these texts in a single volume.

Alongside ancient monasticism and primitive liturgies, another field of interest for him were the patristics literature. It has been said that ever since Anba Epiphanius joined the monastery, he had been encouraged by Father Matthew the Poor to deepen his knowledge of Tradition and the Fathers of the Church. Obedient to his spiritual father, the young monk diligently studied the classical works of patristics and the history of dogma. This is how he began to appreciate the theological and spiritual richness of the Alexandrian Fathers.

In particular, his interest in patristics was intertwined with his interest in Arab-Christian literature. In fact, he dedicated himself to commenting on texts by a thirteenth-century bishop, Būlus al-Būšī, one of the great Egyptian theological authors who wrote in Arabic. For him, this author represented the natural extension of the golden age of the ancient Greek-speaking Alexandrian patristic tradition, and the link

CHAPTER 6

between the latter and the Arabized Coptic Church. Anba Epiphanius was surprised to find at the heart of the Middle Ages a bishop who knew how to preserve the theological richness of Alexandria despite all the pitfalls suffered by the Church in that difficult era, including language and culture change, oppression, and cultural and material impoverishment. Bishop Būlus al-Būšī was so imbued with Alexandrian patristic texts that he was able to render them in Arabic quasi-verbatim. More than once in the homilies for the Easter, Nativity, and Theophany feasts, Anba Epiphanius presented quotes of Būlus al-Būšī corresponding to those of Saint Athanasius or Saint Cyril. Although primarily a passionate theologian, Anba Epiphanius worked tirelessly in the field of philology to restore an Arabic text faithful to the best manuscripts.

As always, he gave great importance to the manuscripts present in our monastery, or those smuggled out to western libraries, since he believed it was necessary, as a Macarian monk, to offer the texts that the long tradition of our monastery had elaborated, as a genuine expression of a local philological and theological tradition, extended over the centuries. Of Būlus al-Būšī, Anba Epiphanius has published the commentary on the Apocalypse (2017)[6] and the

---

[6] For the English translation, see Bulus al-Bushi, *Commentary*

homilies for the divine feasts (2018).

Bishop Būlus al-Būšī represented, for Anba Epiphanius, a fortunate exception in an exegetical, theological, and spiritual context in which the distance that separates the Coptic Church of that time from that of its origins is increasingly evident. In particular, the work on the Fathers and on this medieval author led Anba Epiphanius to understand the distance that separates today's Church of Alexandria from its original theology. One of the main causes of this detachment is represented by the transition from Coptic to Arabic and the consequent cultural and intellectual discontinuity. More than once, he had listened to his spiritual father explain how Copts had lost our tongue twice, though certainly not immediately, but gradually. Anba Epiphanius used to repeat that the first time was due to the Council of Chalcedon (AD 451), where Copts started to lose Greek, and the second time was due to the arrival of the Arabs (AD 640), where we began to lose the Coptic language, and we became like children who no longer know their parents' language. This realization explains why Anba Epiphanius spent so much energy perfecting his knowledge of ancient Greek and why,

---

on the Apocalypse (Wādī al-Naṭrūn: St. Macarius Press, 2023). The volume is preceded by a rich introduction written by the editor and translator Shady Kiryakos Nessim.

CHAPTER 6

having become abbot, he encouraged his monks to study Greek and other ancient languages.

Scripture represents another work field of Anba Epiphanius. In an attempt to recover the Greek and Coptic roots of the Coptic Church, he worked with great passion on translating the Scripture from Greek and Coptic into Arabic. He began undertaking the Arabic translation of the Septuagint for the Old Testament, offering the Greek text in parallel, as he realized that the Arabic translation offered by Van Dyck, the most widespread edition of the Bible in use by the Coptic church, is based on the Masoretic text, and not on the text that the Fathers used to read. It is a venture of a great scientific and spiritual standing that materialized with translations of the books of Genesis, Exodus, and Isaiah, the latter of which was released posthumously at the end of February 2020. Furthermore, he had encouraged other monks of his monastery to do likewise.

His academic passion also explains the unconditional support and generous help he offered to young Coptic institutions interested in theological and patristic studies, such as *Alexandria School* and the *Holy Transfiguration College* of which he was president of the scientific committee. *Agora University* greeted the abbot of Saint Macarius' monastery with these words:

> His Grace fulfilled his advisory role at Agora University with such a high level of integrity, without concern for

building a name or legacy for himself, but rather embracing a prayerful approach of serving the collective Body of Christ.[7]

His Holiness Pope Tawadros II had also asked him to follow *Mu'assat al-Qiddīs Marqus li-Tawṯīq al-Turāṯ* (St Mark Foundation for the Documentation of the Heritage) which mainly deals with the study of Coptic history through the organization of conferences and the publication of scientific texts of historical interest. Naglā Ḥamdī, a scholar at the *Institut Français d'Archéologie Orientale*, recalls:

> I attended meetings of [Saint Mark] Foundation with him and was amazed when I saw how consistently he attended these meetings. He always arrived early, making a long journey. When asked to sit at the head of the table, he used to decline with a mild smile. If someone insisted, he tried to justify himself by saying, 'I'll remain here because air conditioning does not reach there.' At the meetings, he listened carefully to everyone, taking notes. When we asked him to express his opinion, he asked for permission to do so. Truly, as the Scripture says, 'The mouth of the righteous meditates on wisdom and his tongue speaks the truth' (Ps. 37:30). Everyone marveled at that wisdom.[8]

---

[7] http://aui.ac/hgbe (accessible only through Wayback Machine in *archive.org*).

[8] *A Face*: 42.

CHAPTER 6

Pope Tawadros II had nominated Anba Epiphanius to become a member of the board of directors of the *Markaz al-Dirāsāt al-Qibṭiyya* (Center of Coptic Studies) of the *Bibliotheca Alexandrina*, the first Egyptian governmental organization interested in the cultural aspects of Coptic heritage. The center also launched a new scientific journal *Coptica Alexandrina*.[9] The director of the center, Lu'ay Sa'id, remembered the Coptic bishop in a national magazine:

> Monk Epiphanius (this was the title he loved even after becoming bishop) always attended conferences… and was always meek, of few words, simple, extremely humble. Nevertheless, he was intellectually a giant and amazed those around him with his analysis of great caliber, breadth of vision, encyclopedic knowledge in numerous fields, as well as mastery of numerous living and ancient languages.[10]

2. *His Care for Egyptian Monasteries*

Anba Epiphanius had the monasteries at heart. Pope Tawadros II entrusted him with the organization of three seminars in Egypt focusing on monastic life, both for monks and nuns (from 2015 to 2017). In addition to this, he was tasked with the difficult

---

[9] See the journal's website, https://www.bibalex.org/coptica (accessed: July 14, 2023).

[10] Lu'ay Sa'īd, "Widā'an Ṣadīqī al-'Usquf" [Goodbye friend bishop], in *Rose al-Yūsuf*, August 22, 2018.

mission of creating a theological school for monks, and he was actively working to bring the project to light prior to his departure. There are numerous episodes that highlight his desire to help bring Coptic monasteries back to being the theological breeding ground they once were. He once told a brother how he toured the nuns' convents of Old Cairo, handing the nun at the door of each monastery a copy of his publications, introducing himself simply as "a monk of Saint Macarius." Father Seraphim al-Baramusi tells how, once, a nun asked him from which sources to start studying theology. After some thought, Anba Epiphanius invited her to read good translations of patristic, liturgical, and monastic texts. The nun confessed that such publications were difficult to obtain. Then the bishop promised her to send to each of their monasteries an entire theological, liturgical, biblical, and monastic digital library. He then later expressed to Father Seraphim al-Baramūsī:

> Monasteries must absolutely have all the sources, and monks must be encouraged to read and research because it is from monasteries that Orthodox theology is born.[11]

---

[11] *A Face*: 59.

CHAPTER 6

3. Support for Young Scholars

There are many young scholars whom Anba Epiphanius helped obtain a scholarship or encouraged to continue their studies in theology or patristics. For him, young scholars represented the hope of a renewal of the Church, which, in the future, will thus have strengthened its bonds of communion with the spiritual and theological richness of its past. Naglā' Ḥamdī writes:

> Anba Epiphanius, this humble scholar with encyclopedic knowledge, has always encouraged everyone to research and learn, especially the young people. He encouraged young researchers to open up to others and learn foreign languages in order to always be up to date with scientific production.[12]

4. Ecclesiological and Theological Vision

Having surveyed the fields of interest that were close to his heart, it is not difficult to discover the beating center that influenced them all.

Anba Epiphanius had a profound *sensus Ecclesiae*, which is a sense of communion. Certainly, the central nucleus of the Anba Epiphanius' ecclesiological vision was represented by the profound communion that unites the Body of Christ, or the Church. In his studies, he had delved into the concept of the Church-

---

[12] *A Face*: 40.

ANBA EPIPHANIUS' UNIVERSE

Body of Christ in the Fathers' writings. He had learned from the works by Mersch,[13] with regards to the Fathers' general perspective on this, and from Du Manoir, for the writings of Saint Cyril of Alexandria in particular.[14] This sharpened his sense of communion even more, extending over time and space. He lived in profound communion with the various generations of monks who had preceded him from the fourth century to the present day, explaining his great love for the monastic tradition.

Communion over time also explains his interest in ancient liturgies in their original languages. In studying them, he could enter into communion with the liturgical assemblies of all those who had passed. The Eucharist is a factor of communion, not only for us contemporaries, but even more throughout the centuries, "For we, though many, are one bread and one body; for we all partake of that one bread" (1 Cor. 10:17). He himself highlighted the fact that the study of liturgical texts, in their primitive forms, could help the Coptic Church increase theological and spiritual self-awareness. Such self-awareness could not fail to produce a further space of communion with the

---

[13] Emile Mersch, *The Whole Christ: The Historical Development of the Doctrine of the Mystical Body in Scripture and Tradition* (Milwaukee, WI: The Bruce Publishing Company, 1938).

[14] Hubert du Manoir de Juaye, *Dogme et spiritualité chez saint Cyrille d'Alexandrie* (Paris: Librairie Philosophique Brin, 1944).

CHAPTER 6

katholikē ekklēsia, the universal Church. In fact, he wrote:

> With the progress of ecumenical dialogues between the Churches in order to achieve unity, perhaps our liturgical texts in the original Greek can represent the nucleus and the foundation from which to illustrate the authenticity of the Orthodox teaching that we have received from the Church Fathers.[15]

Undoubtedly, the Church as communion over time also explains his interest in the Church Fathers and the richness of their theology, in particular Bishop Būlus al-Būsī, as previously outlined. For Anba Epiphanius, Būlus al-Būsī embodied a communion over time despite the linguistic, cultural, and theological discontinuity. In this sense, Būlus al-Būsī represented exactly what Anba Epiphanius wished to be in his time: a *homo communionis*. And he also encouraged others to become like him.

It is important to note that Anba Epiphanius' interest in patristics shows that his strong ecclesiological vision has its roots in an equally strong theological perspective. In this regard, he often explained to different audiences (e.g., in Bayāḍ, Egypt, January 2018, and Melbourne, Australia, July 17, 2018) how this doctrine of the Church as Body of Christ had been

---

[15] Anba Epiphanius, *al-Ḥulāǧī al-Muqaddas, al-Quddāsāt al-Ṯalāṯa* [The Holy Euchologion: The Three Anaphoras] (Cairo: Madrasat al-Iskandariyya, 2017): 8.

ANBA EPIPHANIUS' UNIVERSE

central to Saint Paul, and how it is inextricably linked to the phrase that was the cause of the conversion of the Apostle, "Saul, Saul, why are you persecuting me?" (Acts 9:4). For Anba Epiphanius, Saint Paul began to understand the mystery of Christ—or the mystery of God and the mystery of man, the purpose of creation, the "dispensation of the fullness of the times" (Eph. 1:10)—at the very moment in which he realized the very close relationship, or rather, the existential relationship that exists between the Lord and those men and women whom he persecuted. They and Jesus—who spoke to him on the road to Damascus and who represented the center of the light in which he was immersed—constituted a single entity. The nucleus of the theological teaching, from which all Anba Epiphanius' ecclesiology sprang, was *being-in-Christ*, our living in Christ, and the living of Christ in us. In this, he was a faithful disciple of Father Matthew the Poor's theology.

In fact, we read in Father Matthew the Poor:

Faith in Christ has two plans: the intelligent, rational human level that understands the reality of the Lord God, which can be the subject of books, conversations, and long talks on the divine essence; we see it from afar and talk about it. The second plan is the spiritual plan that, through the awareness of the soul, sees and senses the "Lord Spirit," not as if He were another, but in the sense in which the ego vanishes, that is, the self—'I also count all things loss for the excellence of the

CHAPTER 6

knowledge of Christ Jesus my Lord, for whom I have suffered the loss of all things, and count them as rubbish, that I may gain Christ and be found in Him' (Phil. 3:8-9). It is clear from Saint Paul's words that he lost all things, and there was nothing left for him but Christ! Christ is the one who filled his being and conscience, so he no longer thinks or feels anything except in Christ. Saint Paul's faith in Christ made Christ everything for him, even his very person. This spiritual awareness of the person of Christ, who fills all, cannot be understood by the mind at all, because the mind perceives what is other than itself and does not comprehend itself. On the contrary, the spiritual faith in Christ made Christ my own self. I am no longer another for Christ and Christ is no longer another for me, 'But he who is joined to the Lord is one spirit with Him' (1 Cor. 6:17).[16]

This mutual indwelling of Christ in believers, this physical union between God and human beings in the Lord Jesus, was not theoretical for Anba Epiphanius but represented an objective fact, so concrete and real as to have direct consequences on the spiritual life and morals of every Christian. In Anba Epiphanius' theological vision, the mystical union with Christ was the center of the Christian's life. It was so important to him that he often said, "without this

---

[16] Mattā al-Miskīn, *al-Ḥilqa al-Ǧadīda lil-Insān Fī al-Īmān al-Masīḥī* [The New Creation of Man in the Christian Faith] (Wādī al-Naṭrūn: Saint Macarius Monastery, 1997): 130.

mystical union, our Christian life has no value." Father Seraphim al-Baramūsī states:

> He loved to repeat 'we are in Christ' as if it were a little prayer through which he brought out a hidden strength in his heart and produced a gleam in his face and in his eyes... I believe I never sat with him without him pronouncing the words, "We are in Christ!" It was almost as if he revealed a completely new mystery that amazed him and filled him with gratitude towards the Lord Jesus. This ardor of his resembled that of the martyr Ignatius of Antioch, who wrote, 'Only [in one way or another] let us be found in Christ Jesus unto the true life. Apart from Him, let nothing attract you' (*Letter to the Ephesians*, 11:1-2).[17]

We read in one of Anba Epiphanius' catechesis:

> Christ is the new divine space that embraces and pervades us. We now live in Him. If we do not understand this truth with our spirit (and not with our mind)... election, adoption, redemption, and recapitulation will remain theoretical concepts that we will not be able to grasp or understand spiritually, since all these things have been accomplished and given to us *in Christ*.[18]

The abbot of Saint Macarius' Monastery attempted to explain this 'new divine space' with a metaphor borrowed from Saint Macarius, who, in turn, made it

---

[17] *A Face*: 53-4.
[18] Anba Epiphanius, "Risālat Ifisus al-'Iṣḥāḥ al-'Awwal" [Epistle to the Ephesians, First Chapter], in *A Face*: 317.

CHAPTER 6

his own by listening to Saint Antonius. In one of his famous apothegms, the father of monks said:

> Just as fish die if they are on dry land for some time, so do monks who loiter outside their cells or waste time with worldlings release themselves from the tension of hesychia. So we should hasten back to the cell (like the fish to the sea) lest while loitering outside, we forget to keep a watch on the inner [self.].[19]

Saint Macarius transposed the metaphor onto a theological and soteriological level by saying:

> A fish cannot live out of the water... so without the Lord Jesus, and the energy of his divine power, no one can know the mysteries and wisdom of God, or be rich and a Christian.[20]

Taking up the spirit of these two texts, Anba Epiphanius wrote:

> When a fish lives in the sea, it can swim or stop somewhere. Yet all its movements take place within the water that surrounds it on all sides. Aquatic organisms are completely covered by water. In Christianity, this applies to us. Whether I am in the church or outside the church, next to the altar taking communion, or in the central nave, whether I am at work or at home, I am like the fish that lives inside this space. I live in a space where Christ is present at all times. If I continually think about the idea that 'I am in Christ,' I am protected

---

[19] *Alphabetical Collection*, Anthony 10 (*Alphabetical*: 33).
[20] Macarius, *Fifty Spiritual Homilies* 17:10.

from so many sins and so many problems. Even if I fall into sin, I immediately perceive that I am united with Him and that He is in me and I in Him.[21]

Now it is possible to better understand how his interest in the Fathers was linked to deep theological motivations. For Anba Epiphanius, the process of the *théōsis*, or deification, of Christians, about which the Fathers, especially the Alexandrian ones, abundantly speak,[22] is precisely one of the main spiritual consequences of the Incarnation of God and of our living *in Christ*. It is through His uniting Himself to our nature—His taking us into Him—that Christ accomplished our redemption and opened up for us the possibility of uniting ourselves with Him. It is by uniting ourselves to Him—by receiving Him within us—that we receive the effects of this redemption and are made partakers of the divine nature (cf. 2 Pet. 1:4). Anba Epiphanius is one of the theologians who worked towards a gradual reconciliation with the concept of *théōsis*. It is known, in fact, that the Coptic Church refused the doctrine of divinization in the years preceding Pope Tawadros, considering it a heretical theology.[23] Today, the seed planted by Father

---

[21] *A Face*: 54.

[22] Norman Russell, *The Doctrine of Deification in the Greek Patristic Tradition* (Oxford: Oxford University Press, 2006).

[23] Pope Shenouda III, *Bida' Ḥadīta* [Modern Heresies] (Cairo: al-Kulliyya al-Iklīrīkiyya bil-'Abbāsiyya, 2006): 141-174.

CHAPTER 6

Matthew the Poor—who always defended this theology not only as Christian but also authentically 'Alexandrian'—and his spiritual son, begins to bear fruit.

One day, a bishop confided to Anba Epiphanius the difficulty of accepting *theōsis*. The problem for that bishop—as for many Copts today—was, on the one hand, how it is possible to reconcile *theōsis* with our creatureliness; on the other, how is it possible to reconcile it with the sin we continually commit? The answer he received from Anba Epiphanius was:

> It is difficult for us to accept *theōsis* because we do not live holiness. Those who live holiness do not consider a similar concept strange since they are aware of the deep existential bond that binds them to God and perceive this communion with God within themselves. How can those who live in a 'quagmire' accept such a concept that they have never experienced inside themselves? It is the life of holiness that is the gateway to understanding theology, and not vice versa. Experience is the foundation of the reception of theological sense. When experience is poor, it results in a poor acceptance of theological truths and our inheritance in Christ, which instead are characterized by great richness.[24]

Another source, who was present when Anba Epiphanius said these words and who wishes to

---

[24] Dialogue quoted by Father Seraphim al-Baramūsī in *A Face*: 65.

ANBA EPIPHANIUS' UNIVERSE

remain anonymous, recounted that the abbot exemplified the question by speaking of the children of the King and the children of this world:

> Unlike the children of this world who roll around in the mud and remain there, the King's children, even if they get dirty, get up, shake off the mud, wash themselves, put on their royal clothes, and go back to enjoying the embrace of their Father.

By saying this, Anba Epiphanius uses a typical image of Saint Macarius, who spoke of Christ as a mother:

> A brother asked Abba Macarius, "My father, I have committed a transgression." Abba Macarius said to him, "It is written, my child, 'I do not desire the death of a sinner so much as his repentance and his life'. Repent, therefore, my child; you will see him who is gentle, our Lord Jesus Christ, his face full of joy for you, like a nursing mother whose face is full of joy for her child. When he raises his hands and his face up to her, even if he is full of all kinds of uncleanness, she does not turn away from that bad smell and excrement but takes pity on him and lifts him up and presses him to her breast, her face full of joy, and everything about him is sweet to her. If then, this created person has pity for her child, how much greater is the love of the creator, our Lord Jesus Christ, for us!"[25]

---

[25] *Virtues of Macarius*, 23 (*Spiritbearer*: 104).

CHAPTER 6

At the end of this speech, the bishop who questioned him replied, "If divinization means this, then we all believe it!"

Anba Epiphanius' ethical and moral perspective also derives from being *in Christ*. For him, ethical and moral values in Christianity do not derive from pedagogical or social principles, but from the heart of our communion and union with Christ. As he affirms in one of his famous catechesis, Christian ethics is 'in the Lord' and not only 'for the Lord,' or 'to please the Lord' or 'out of fear of the Lord.' This means that human action, especially in the ecclesial space, is dictated by the fact that Christians are all members of the one Body of the Lord. Indeed, just as the members submit to one another in perfect harmony for the good of the whole body, so it is necessary that Christians submit to one another for the good of the Body of Christ and for love of Him to whom the Body belongs. It is therefore understandable why sectarianism, division, and dispersion that Anba Epiphanius always condemned in his life, especially in the period in which he became a public figure, constitute one of the gravest sins, since they strike at the heart the cohesion of the Body of Christ.

5. *His Vision Concerning the Church Unity*

It is in this theological and ecclesiological perspective—the profound sense of communion that animated Anba Epiphanius—that his openness and love for the Christians of the other Churches must also be read. Anba Epiphanius had understood and tried to teach those he met that the Church, the Body of Christ, cannot be divided and that, despite the walls and barriers created by men, there is a deep communion between the different members of the Body of Christ as an underground aquifer. It was this conviction that guided him in all his relationships with Christians from other churches; a conviction expressed on the occasion of a conference attended by Christians of different churches in this way:

> Here there are people who are not officially in communion, who call the others 'brothers and sisters' from the tribune. What brotherhood do they mean? If they mean the one inaugurated by Christ and do not seriously seek the unity of the Body of the Church, then they are liars!'[26]

Undoubtedly, he was predisposed to encounter those who were different from him by his natural openness of spirit, vast culture, respect for the opinions of others, and innate delicacy. This is why Pope Tawadros II asked him, about twenty times, to represent the Coptic Church in various symposiums and ecumenical conferences. He always honored the Church by presenting a faithful and loving image. In

---

[26] *So Great*: 301.

CHAPTER 6

this context, his great respect for the Church of Rome should be remembered. Perhaps it is no coincidence that two months after his ordination, his first journey as a bishop was part of the delegation that accompanied Pope Tawadros II on his first apostolic visit to Rome to meet Pope Francis in 2013.

Anba Epiphanius made many of the reflections of his teacher and spiritual Father Matthew the Poor on the unity of the Church his own. For both of them, reaching a perfect theological consensus does not happen in the context of ecumenical dialogues that may one day lead to unity. Rather, unity must first be lived then discussed, and it is then that it will become a reality.

Father Matthew wrote:

> Human logic dictates that the distinctions be removed first for unity to take place. As expressed through divine inspiration, God's logic requires that unity be accomplished first, so that the middle wall of separation can be broken down (cf. Eph. 2:14).[27]

For this reason, in all his meetings, Anba Epiphanius was attentive to living in unity and the communion of love with his conversers, more than discussing it with them. One day, while he was having lunch at the Monastery of Bose, in Italy, with other

---

[27] Matthew the Poor, *The Mystery of Unity* (Wādī al-Naṭrūn: St Macarius Press, forthcoming).

bishops representing their own respective churches, he said:

> We are now sitting here, all together, and we are eating food that we all believe has been sanctified by our common prayer. I wonder then: what prevents us from communicating together to the Body and Blood of Christ?'[28]

He confided to a monk of the Monastery of Bose:

> When a baptized Christian presents himself to me to receive the Body of Christ, and believes in truth that it is the Body of Christ, I have no right to refuse it to him.[29]

Although possessing this boundless horizon, his *sensus Ecclesiae* ensured that he respected the decisions of the synod of bishops of his Church. Whenever he had to decide whether or not to give communion to a Christian whose church was not officially in communion with the Coptic Orthodox Church, he suffered a terrible inner laceration.

In particular, in the context of ecumenical dialogue, which sadly he often interpreted as a dialogue between deaf people, for Anba Epiphanius it was essential to distinguish between dogma (what was common to the undivided Church), *theologumenon* (theological opinion), and interpretation of dogma

---

[28] *So Great*: 298.
[29] *Ibid.*: 27.

CHAPTER 6

(the diversity of theological perspectives that have characterized the various Fathers and the various Churches over the centuries, and which do not affect the essential aspect of the faith).[30] It is therefore necessary to converge on what is essential about dogma by discussing and commenting on one's own *theologumena* together, without becoming rigid in them or, worse still, expecting others to fully assume our interpretations of dogma. Although this distinction is currently rather rare in the Coptic theological environment, without it, there is the risk of demanding from others something that they are incapable of offering, thus blocking efforts towards unity. The common doctrinal basis, i.e., the core of the faith around which to converge, was, according to Anba Epiphanius, the Nicean-Constantinople Creed.

In this, he did not invent anything new in the Coptic sphere. In fact, he referred to a whole Coptic canonical tradition according to which the Nicean-Constantinople Creed was sufficient to establish the orthodoxy of the faith.[31]

---

[30] Convinced of the central importance of this distinction, he repeatedly spoke about it before different audiences (monks, priests, lay people), both in Egypt and abroad (Austria, Australia). The summary of his perspective can be read in Anba Epiphanius, "al-'Aqīda wa-l-ra'y wa-l-tafsīr" [Dogma, Theologumenon, and Exegesis] in *A Face*: 187-197.

[31] Cf. Anba Epiphanius, "Ṭaqs al-Inḍimām lil-Kanīsa al-Qibṭiyya Ḥasab Maḫṭūṭāt al-'Uṣūr al-Wusṭā" [The Liturgical

ANBA EPIPHANIUS' UNIVERSE

Father Seraphim al-Baramūsī writes:

He was never a bishop who sat down with someone different from him in faith to give him a lesson in orthodoxy! Absolutely not. He sought with the other what was common to both, striving to find points of contact together and establishing together a theological language that was in harmony with the roots of the ancient Church. In this way, he gained everyone and obtained everyone's respect. Even when he disagreed with someone, the bridges created by love represented the icon he wanted to appear clear in front of everyone. He seemed to say, yes, we can love each other despite diversity.[32]

Another fundamental point for Anba Epiphanius was that it was necessary, indeed indispensable, to reread one's own ecclesial history with a critical eye. One cannot intransigently accept positions of *yesterday* that led to separation at the expense of a communion that the Lord Himself insistently demands of

---

Practices of Joining the Coptic Church According to Medieval Manuscripts] in *A Face:* 465-480. A well-documented study of the historical development of the issue of rebaptism and the acceptance of holy orders of other Churches within the Early Church and the Church of Alexandria was presented in Melbourne in 2017: Anba Epiphanius, "Ṭarḥ Ḥawla Mas'alat Qubūl al-Kanīsa al-Qibṭiyya al-'Urṯūḏuksiyya lil-Ma'mūdiyya Allatī Tatimm Ḫāriğahā" [Presentation of the Question of the Acceptance by the Coptic Orthodox Church of Baptism That is Administered Outside of It], in *A Face:* 441-462.

[32] *A Face*: 61-62.

CHAPTER 6

us *today*—"May all be *one* in us... so that the world may believe" (John 17:21). For Anba Epiphanius—if we remain in the context of communion in space and time—positions and rigidities that have led to the rupture of this communion does not make sense. To open up to true communion and acquire a critical spirit capable of discerning one's mistakes, one is required to deny his ecclesial ego, just as in the personal sphere we are asked to deny our ego, according to the Lord's command. For Anba Epiphanius, it was unfair that *today* we had to pay the price for *yesterday*'s unresolved conflicts and quarrels, created by holy but certainly not infallible men. Infallibility, for Anba Epiphanius, is specific only to Jesus Christ, the only One without sin (cf. Heb. 4:15). He said:

> We cannot justify or rationally interpret [yesterday's conflicts] today except as conflicts about who was the greatest (cf. Mark 9:34-37).

[33] For him, it was therefore necessary to lighten *yesterday*'s ballast in order to be able to run forward more quickly *today*, according to the words of the Apostle, "forgetting those things which are behind and reaching forward to those things which are ahead" (Phil. 3:13).

During the first apostolic visit of Pope Francis to Egypt, a joint declaration was presented, which Pope

---

[33] *A Face*: 439-440.

ANBA EPIPHANIUS' UNIVERSE

Tawadros and Pope Francis signed together in Cairo on April 28, 2017. The declaration, on which Anba Epiphanius collaborated, said, among other things:

> Today we, Pope Francis and Pope Tawadros II, in order to please the heart of the Lord Jesus, as well as that of our sons and daughters in the faith, mutually declare that we, with one mind and heart, will seek sincerely not to repeat the baptism that has been administered in either of our Churches for any person who wishes to join the other.[34]

This phrase, misinterpreted by the more conservative Coptic circles, who saw it as a sort of antechamber to the imminent and total re-establishment of communion between the two churches, gave rise to numerous controversies. In response to the controversies that were struggling to subside, Anba Epiphanius delivered a speech on the occasion of the twenty-sixth conference of the Center for Studies on Middle Eastern Christianity of the Theological Faculty of the Evangelical Church in Cairo (February 22-24, 2018), in which he offered a historical perspective on the question. By employing three Copto-

---

[34] The text was published both by the Coptic Orthodox Church (in Arabic) in the official journal of the Patriarchate (*al-Kirāza*, year 45, n. 17-18, May 5, 2017, pp. 6-7; available online: https://tinyurl.com/kiraza200505 (accessed: January 2023)), and by the Roman Catholic Church (in various languages) on its official website (https://tinyurl.com/commondec).

CHAPTER 6

Arabic manuscripts, he exposed the canons of three hierarchs of the Coptic Church of the 11th, 13th and 15th centuries and was able to demonstrate how the Coptic Orthodox Church had, in the past, accepted the baptism of the Christians of other Churches as valid, and how even the repetition of the anointing with the holy myron had not always been practiced.[35]

To a young Catholic monk who asked him about how it was possible to move ecumenical dialogue in the sense of concrete steps towards unity, Anba Epiphanius replied:

> In ecumenical dialogues, we cannot expect to come to think of it all in the same way. It is necessary to distinguish between dogma and theological opinion. I mean, do we all believe in the Trinity? Well! Then if I interpret the Trinity in one way and the other in another, it can be the object of dialogue, but it cannot prevent us from being united. We are talking about theological hypotheses. The Fathers of the Church themselves diverged on this point. I will give you another example. At the beginning of Christianity, there were two heresies: one believed in the Trinity and the other did not; one baptized in the name of the Trinity and the other in the name of Jesus. At Nicaea the baptism of the first was accepted because it was conferred in the name of

---

[35] The paper can be viewed in its entirety on Youtube at the following address: https://youtu.be/nBL7N1cP4hM (accessed: July 14, 2023).

the Trinity, despite their being heretical on other issues.[36]

The brother replied:

Yes, but how do you see the question of the infallibility of the Church? For us Catholics, for instance, it is clear that the Council of Vatican I is a problem, and yet no one will ever dream of openly admitting that at that juncture the Church gathered in council confused the truth with error.[37]

Anba Epiphanius replied:

Yet the Church can make mistakes. The great problem faced by the churches today is the ecclesial ego. The last Catholic popes have made a very important gesture by asking for forgiveness. And asking for forgiveness is admitting that you were wrong, and therefore recognizing the fallibility of the Church. Furthermore, we must always ask ourselves what we are looking for. Are we really looking for unity or not? You know well that it is even possible to make the Bible say something and its exact opposite. Everything depends on what we are looking for. The same applies to the statements of the Church. If we truly want unity, we will find words of unity, and everything else will take a second place.[38]

---

[36] *So Great*: 299-300.
[37] *Ibid*.
[38] *Ibid*.

CHAPTER 6

"Everything depends on what we are looking for". Anba Epiphanius once remarked in an unofficial dialogue at the Pro Oriente foundation in Vienna:

> I personally believe that perhaps the greatest obstacle to unity between the churches is the lack of will on the part of those responsible for dialogue to bring about such unity.[39]

In a report of the meeting in which he expressed this opinion, Anba Epiphanius stressed the need to accept the great diversity that exists in the Church:

> We must start from diversity. We must consider ourselves different and not heretics. If we start from the fact that we consider each other heretics, we will achieve very little.[40]

The abbot of the Monastery of Saint Macarius also participated, as a speaker, in ten international and numerous national conferences. In fact, the last thing he was working on a few hours before his death was a paper that focused on discernment in the lives of the Desert Fathers, intended for the International Ecumenical Conference of Orthodox Spirituality, which was held in Bose in September 2018 and which he unfortunately did not attend. Anba Epiphanius was also twice invited (in 2016 and 2018) to the sessions

---

[39] *A Face*: 439.
[40] Anba Epiphanius, *Segni di comunione* (in Italian: https://tinyurl.com/segnidicom. Accessed: July 14, 2023).

ANBA EPIPHANIUS' UNIVERSE

of the *Commission for the Ecumenical Encounter between the Eastern Orthodox Churches and the Catholic Church* (CEE), based in Vienna, at the *Pro Oriente* foundation.

In fact, on one occasion, his tireless effort to create communion was admirably summarized as a saying of a father of today's desert. In the Monastery of Bose, following a speech during a conference, the discussion moved to the divisions between the churches, the causes of these divisions, and the possible solutions. Although the discussion became intense among its participants, Anba Epiphanius remained silent. Finally, the moderator said, "Let us hear what the Desert Fathers have to say on this issue." Calling on Anba Epiphanius' perspective, the bishop replied:

> Forgive me, I am not a theologian. I do not understand divisions. I only know what unity is.[41]

A great, liberating applause sealed the wisdom of the desert.

6. His Exegetical Perspective

In Anba Epiphanius' life, Scripture was absolutely central. It represented the indispensable daily nourishment that keeps us constantly united to Christ, through which we grow in the knowledge of Him. To Anba Epiphanius, the linguistic, literary, and

---

[41] *So Great*: 299.

CHAPTER 6

historical background is of fundamental importance in undertaking a serious exegesis that considers the complexity of the text and the context in which God's simplicity is revealed. To do this, Anba Epiphanius used all possible tools. Firstly, the in-depth study of the ancient biblical languages (in particular Hebrew and Greek) was his primary tool for the critical understanding of the scriptural texts. Anba Epiphanius accustomed his monks not to blindly trust any translation of modern languages because any translation, however good, is always limited and experimental. His homilies, though rare, never lacked recourse to the original texts. As he often said of himself, he was not a homilist. He was and remained a serious biblical scholar and this clearly transpired from the pulpit. Anba Epiphanius loved to study and meditate on the use of the single word in its original language. For him, it was essential to arrive to a precise understanding of the letter of the text in order to understand its spirit.

Another defining characteristic of the Coptic bishop was his great respect and love for the Old Testament. In the background of his speeches with a New Testament flavor there is almost always the Old Testament without which one would not understand "so great a salvation" (Heb. 2:3) accomplished by Christ. However, he always used the Old Testament as a premise—certainly necessary but still a premise—

ANBA EPIPHANIUS' UNIVERSE

for the announcement of the fulfillment of salvation by the Lord and for the transmission of this salvation to us. God's assumption of our human nature, His life-giving death and His glorious resurrection are the exegetical key of all Scripture since Christ, the *Theanthropos*, is the *alpha* and *omega*, the center of everything. We—we dare to say—are at the heart of the Heart of everything. We are the recipients of all that the Lord, in His great goodness, has done and continues to do.

Furthermore, despite his approach of great scientific seriousness, which meant that he was not afraid, for example, of contemporary critical exegetical studies, Anba Epiphanius always tried to place his own exegetical research within the framework of Tradition with a capital 'T,' resorting both to patristical exegesis, in particular to the Alexandrian Fathers, as well as to the liturgical practice of the Church, in particular the Coptic liturgy.

In this sense, the exegetical activity of Anba Epiphanius is at the crossroads of two other fields in which he worked a great deal: patristics and liturgy. For him, the Scripture must be studied and read critically in order to be understood. However, it is not a simple philological reality. Above all, it remains the living Word of God which must be meditated and ruminated on in the depths of the heart. The spiritual datum certainly remains the center of his research,

CHAPTER 6

since the primacy remains of the Spirit who is the only one to guide the reader towards 'the thought of Christ' (cf. 2 Cor. 10:5), to reveal the mystery of Christ hidden in the lines. For our father the bishop, it was necessary to remain adherent to an ecclesial understanding of Scripture, as it is not a dead letter, but life in action ('The word of God is alive, effective and sharper than any doubled sword cutting,' (Heb. 4:12), a life that is lived within the Church. Once again, we are faced with another manifestation of his deep search for communion. All this means that his exegesis represents an extraordinary encounter between ancient and modern, between consolidated traditional data and new critical perspectives in the philological, historical, literary, philosophical, and archaeological fields. Among other things, it should be noted that many of the exegetical articles published in the periodical of the monastery, *Saint Mark,* were, in their germinal form, only simple notes for personal meditation and for the study of Scripture. Starting from the search for multiple meanings of just a single term, the Spirit disclosed the Scriptures to Anba Epiphanius as one opens a precious casket whose key has been found. It is this biblical and exegetical treasure that Anba Epiphanius managed to deliver to us, before being received into heavenly glory.

CONCLUSION
TWICE A MARTYR,
TWICE A WITNESS

The monastic—and we would say simply Christian—consistency of Anba Epiphanius made him a credible, exceptional witness of Christ. He was, therefore, truly a *martyr* in the Greek etymological sense of the term, which translates to 'witness.' It is interesting then to note that it is with the term 'martyrdom' that the monastic literature often depicts the spiritual struggle that the monks live, a struggle equal, if not even superior, to that faced during the persecutions by the martyrs—Christians who shed their blood for the faith.

In *Bustān al-Ruhbān*, a saying attributed to Pachomius says:[1]

> Do you think that martyrdom consists only of amputating or burning limbs of the body? No! Even in the labor of asceticism, in the blows that come from the demons, and in diseases. He who bears all this with thanksgiving is the martyr. Otherwise, what need was there for Paul the Apostle to write: 'I die every day' (1

---

[1] Apothegm n° 87 in *Bustān*: 56.

CONCLUSION

Cor. 15:31)? He did not actually die every day, but patiently endured what he suffered.

Saint Athanasius wrote to the monks:

> Martyrs have often come to perfection even in a single instant. In the monastic life, instead, through struggles, one undergoes martyrdom for Christ every day, not with blood and flesh, but one fights against the principalities and powers, against the rulers of this world of darkness, against the evil spirits, fighting to the last breath.[2]

Moreover, Saint Athanasius, in his masterpiece 'Life of Anthony' wrote:

> When at last the persecution ceased, and the blessed Bishop Peter had borne his testimony, Anthony departed, and again withdrew to his cell, and was there daily a martyr to his conscience, and contending in the conflicts of faith.[3]

If it is true that Anba Epiphanius lived as a true monk and therefore fully experienced the 'martyrdom of conscience,' it is also true that he was crowned by the supreme martyrdom 'in blood and flesh,' making him perfectly conform to Christ, even in death.

He was therefore twice a martyr and twice a witness, following the Lamb wherever He goes (cf. Rev. 14:4), without ever taking his eyes off Him. And, like

---

[2] Athanasius of Alexandria, *To the Monks* (PG 28,1424C).

[3] Athanasius of Alexandria, *Life of Anthony*, 47 (*NPNF*, 2nd Ser., Vol. IV: 209).

the Apostle Peter, "a witness of the sufferings of Christ," he was also, already in this life, "a partaker of the glory that will be revealed" (cf. 1 Pet. 5:1).

Martyrdom and monasticism, therefore, are one, as well as transfiguration and monasticism. The story of this meek and humble bishop, presents also unmistakable traits of the Transfiguration and the Resurrection. Following in the footsteps of our Lord, there is no transfiguration without each carrying his own cross and drinking his own cup: "You will indeed drink the cup that I drink, and with the baptism I am baptized with you will be baptized" (Mark 10:39). For Christ, the Transfiguration was immediately followed by the announcement of the Passion and by the Cross itself. This means that their profound interconnection on a mystical level reveals that the Cross cannot exist without Transfiguration. The suffering and the pains of trials are only momentary and are not the definitive reality; instead, the truth is that the body is transfigured forever by the power of the Resurrection of the Lord. Our father Epiphanius is the living example of these words. The life of the *staurophore* (Cross-bearer) and *pneumatophore* (Spirit-bearer) Epiphanius demonstrates this widely. This double-luminous martyrdom cannot be without fruit. "Sow many seeds in me, so that I may reap many times more!", said the martyr Gordius.[4] These are not

---

[4] *Gordius*: 63. See p. 11.

CONCLUSION

only his words, but those of all the martyrs, including Anba Epiphanius. He lived by loving his enemies and letting his body be plowed and sown by the sin of others. In recent times, his health had deteriorated due to the opposition that he had to face in the monastery. The last plague, a serious ulcer, like the sweat of Christ in Gethsemane which became drops of blood for the struggle he had entered (cf. Luke 22:44), was the epiphenomenon of his intense spiritual struggle against evil.

Talking about Bishop Epiphanius today means placing the emphasis on man rather than Sabbath (cf. Mk. 2:27), on grace rather than merits, on love rather than legalism, on mercy rather than rigor, on the Holy Spirit rather than dogmatism, on spirit rather than literalism, on Christ-in-us and Christ-in-others, on God's continued condescension rather than an extreme transcendentalism, on mystery rather than scholasticism, on mysticism rather than moralism, on unity rather than division, on universality rather than confessionalism—after an era in which the opposite was emphasized. To speak of Bishop Epiphanius in today's Coptic Church means, simply, to breathe in the infinite space of the Spirit who blows where He wants (cf. John 3:8). It means living as children and no longer as slaves.

As Christians, we should know that the death of the innocent is seed of life. Tertullian wrote in the 2nd/3rd century *semen est sanguis Christianorum*, "the blood [of the martyrs] is the seed of Christians," which can also be translated "the blood of Christians is the seed [of novelty]".[5] This new seed of life must not be understood in a vague metaphorical sense or as a wish, but rather in a concrete way: new life, new beginning. It is as if God, in front of this great love "to the end" (cf. John 13:1), could not deny the martyr anything he asks.

And the grain of wheat, which fell to the ground under the weight of its cross, died. Yet how much harvest! We have begun to put together the harvest of Anba Epiphanius—that purification of monastic life from worldliness, vanity, and pride that he had so much sought after in life—after his terrible death, through the intercession of his innocent blood. And today we perceive in the monastery his paternal protection and his work of intercession in front of Christ, with the *parrhēsía* (cf. 2 Cor. 3:12) proper to the martyrs. The words of the martyr bishop Ignatius of Antioch, then, not only perfectly match those of the just-mentioned martyr Gordius, but it seems to us to hear them on the lips of our abbot:

> Suffer me to become food for the wild beasts, through whose instrumentality it will be granted me to attain to God. I am the wheat of God, and let me be ground by

---

[5] This is how Onorato Tescari translated this phrase in a 1951 Italian edition of Tertullian's *Apologeticum* published by *Società Editrice Internazionale*.

CONCLUSION

the teeth of the wild beasts, that I may be found the pure bread of Christ.[6]

This seed of mildness planted in Saint Macarius' Monastery and irrigated by innocent blood already bears fruit; this wheat of God has already become pure and fragrant bread.

---

[6] Ignatius of Antioch, *Epistle to the Romans*, 4. *ANF*, vol. 1: 203.

Read also from
ST. MACARIUS PRESS

Commentary on the Apocalypse
BULUS AL-BUSHI

The 13th century Egypt saw a circle of Coptic theologians who passionately endeavored toward the revival of the Coptic Orthodox Church. Bishop Bulus al-Bushi was among those notable church treasures, and dedicated much of his effort to biblical exegesis. In this book, readers will gauge one of his largest works entitled "Commentary on the Apocalypse" which presents a dogmatic and pastoral interpretation of the biblical text.

This English translation honors the work of the late Abbot of St Macarius Monastery, **Bishop Epiphanius (1954-2018)**, who published an Arabic edition of al-Bushi's commentary in 2017.

BULUS AL-BUSHI is the 13th-century Coptic Orthodox Bishop of Old Cairo and a prolific writer.

AVAILABLE ON ALL AMAZON STORES, OR ON OUR WEBSITE
www.stmacariuspress.com
info@stmacariuspress.com

Read also from
ST. MACARIUS PRESS

So Great a Salvation
ANBA EPIPHANIUS

*Second Edition Amended
with a Richer Collection of Sayings*

Let those who have been stung by sin and have had its deadly poison spread throughout their body lift their eyes to the One who died once for their sake, Who is now alive and the Life-giver. They shall feel the tremors of a new life running through their inward parts, renewing their thoughts, their affections, their hopes and their desires. The Lord Jesus revealed in His conversation with Nicodemus the mystery of new life which He granted to him and to all who believe in Him; all that remains for us now is to look upon the Lord Jesus in faith. Then, shall we inherit eternal life and taste "so great a salvation" (Heb. 2:3).

AVAILABLE ON ALL AMAZON STORES, OR ON OUR WEBSITE
www.stmacariuspress.com
info@stmacariuspress.com

www.ingramcontent.com/pod-product-compliance
Lightning Source LLC
Chambersburg PA
CBHW060359080526
44583CB00012B/394